# Nuclear Family Fallout

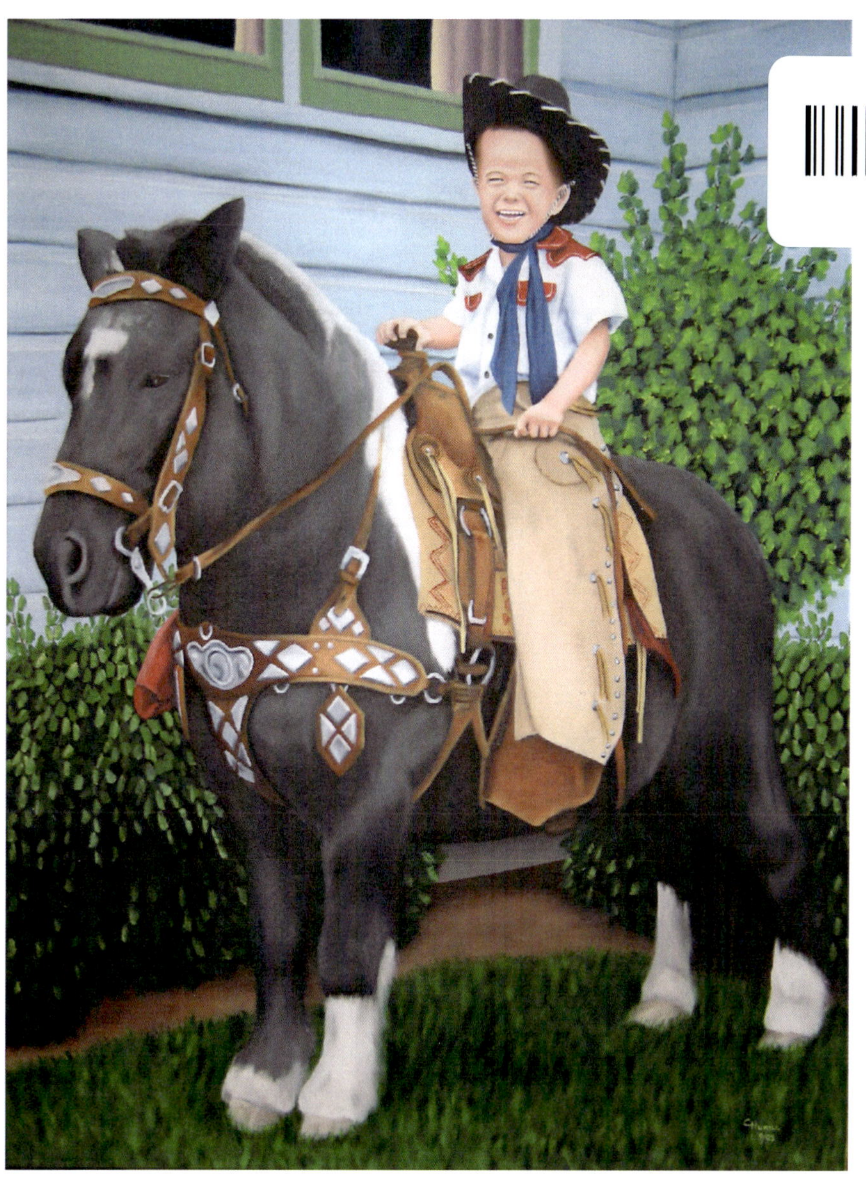

PAINTINGS BY CHARLIE HUKILL

ALL ART WORK © CHARLIE HUKILL

ISBN: 979-8-9873351-3-0

Published by Texas Star Trading Company
174 Cypress Street, Abilene 79601
www.TexasStarTrading.com
(325) 672-9696

Designed by Tinyah Hawkins,
Goofidity Designs

This book is dedicated to my parents, Corinne and Frank Hukill, for their constant love, encouragement, and support and for giving me a set of oil paints in 1966. And to Betty Hukill, my true companion and best friend.

# Foreword

Charlie Hukill is one of the most talented people I know – teaching, acting, directing, designing and building sets, writing plays, inspiring young playwriting students, playing the guitar, and painting in his own distinctive style.

Perhaps Charlie's most distinguishing quality is that he has enriched so many lives in so many positive ways. In addition to being a beloved teacher and confidante, he has been a steadfast, respected leader at McMurry University, at First Central Presbyterian Church, in the Abilene community, and in his profession, as evidenced by his election as president of the Texas Educational Theatre Association.

Charlie cultivates deep and lasting friendships -- because he is loyal and fun and always helpful and encouraging. And his abiding love for Betty, his bride of forty-five-plus years, is truly inspirational.

It is my privilege to introduce, in Charlie's honor and for your reading and viewing pleasure, this unique collection showcasing his incredible talent and his zest, joy, and love of life.

Glenn Dromgoole
Texas Star Trading Company

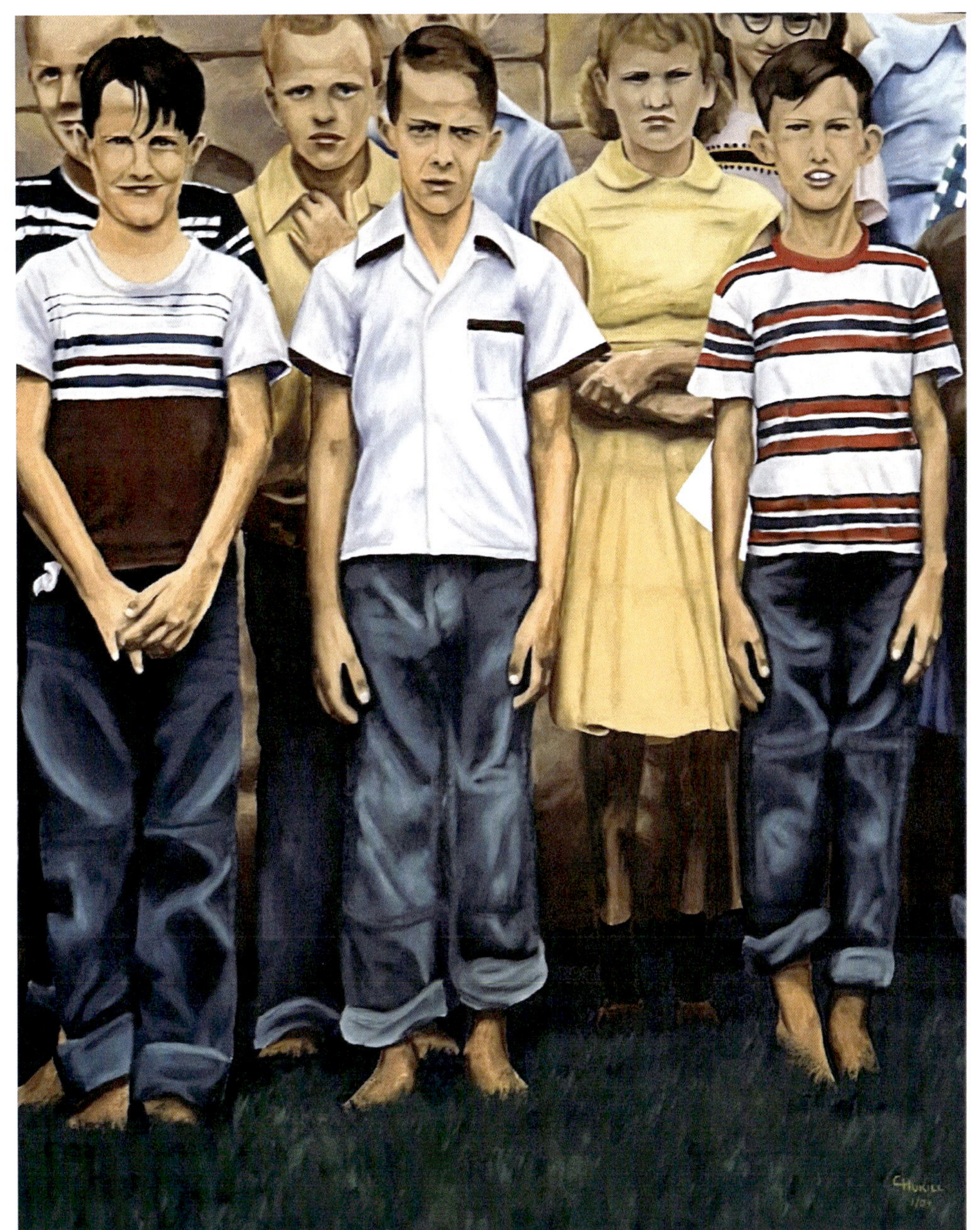

**VBS, 24x30***

Painting used for the cover on Glenn Dromgoole's book, *A Small Town in Texas*.

# Artist's Statement

I don't really like to write about my work as a painter. I just like to paint. I always hope that the work speaks for itself. But, here goes.

My work tends to fall into the traditional representational category. While I sometimes venture in other directions, it always leaves me dissatisfied and I return to the familiar style. I am very much influenced by Edward Hopper and artists of the American Scene.

In particular, I am drawn to images which reflect the era of my childhood, the 1950s, and earlier twentieth century Americana. Many of the paintings included here are of family members or close friends. I derive the greatest pleasure from painting such images.

Paul Baker, the founder and original Artistic Director of the Dallas Theater Center, believed that the artist's creative energy is initially generated in the formative years. In order to create, we must identify and ultimately tap into that original energy source to find inspiration. I agree, and it was this concept that set me on the painting path I have followed. In the mid-eighties, I hit on the "Nuclear Family" theme, which is directly linked to my original creative energy source, and it has been the anchor for my output. I hope that my work inspires a narrative in the respondent and, perhaps, a smile.

I am most grateful to my wife, Betty, for allowing me to have my "studio" set up in our living room and for being my favorite subject matter. I have painted her at least fifteen times over the years, much to her chagrin. I am also grateful to Carol and Glenn Dromgoole for their patronage over the years, their desire to publish this book, but mostly for their friendship.

Charlie Hukill
Abilene, Texas

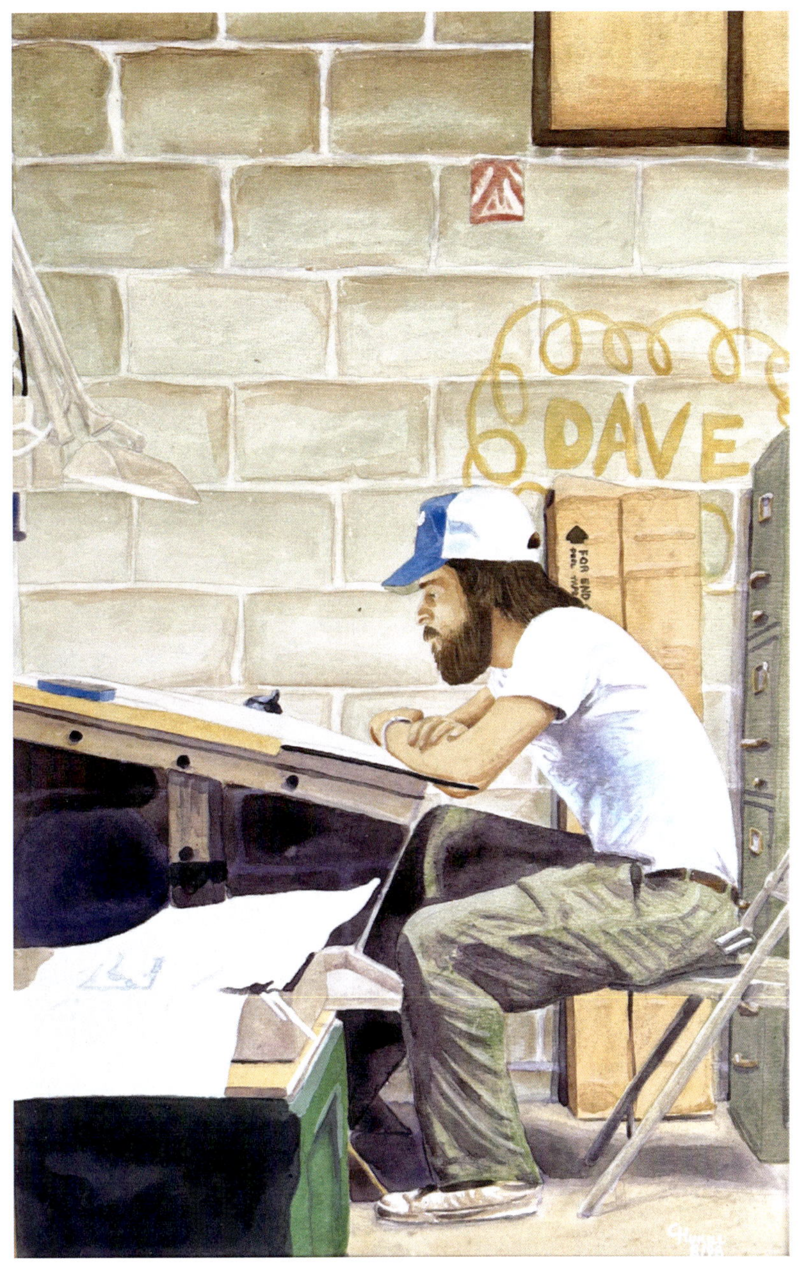


**NOT DAVE, 24X36, ACRYLIC***
Portrait of the artist as a young draftsman.

# Contents



* Designates paintings in private collections.
All paintings in oil unless otherwise indicated.

# Nuclear Family Reunion

Some of these paintings were done as gifts for family members, some decorate my own home. All are very meaningful to me.

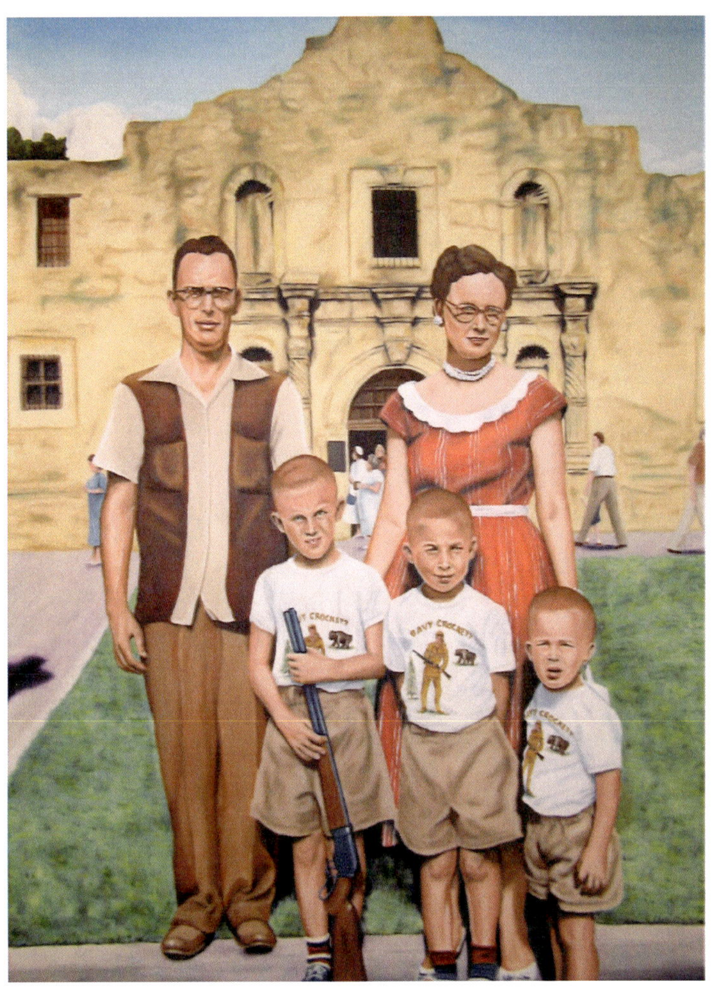

**THE NUCLEAR FAMILY VISITS THE ALAMO, OR TEXAS GOTHIC, 30X40 ***

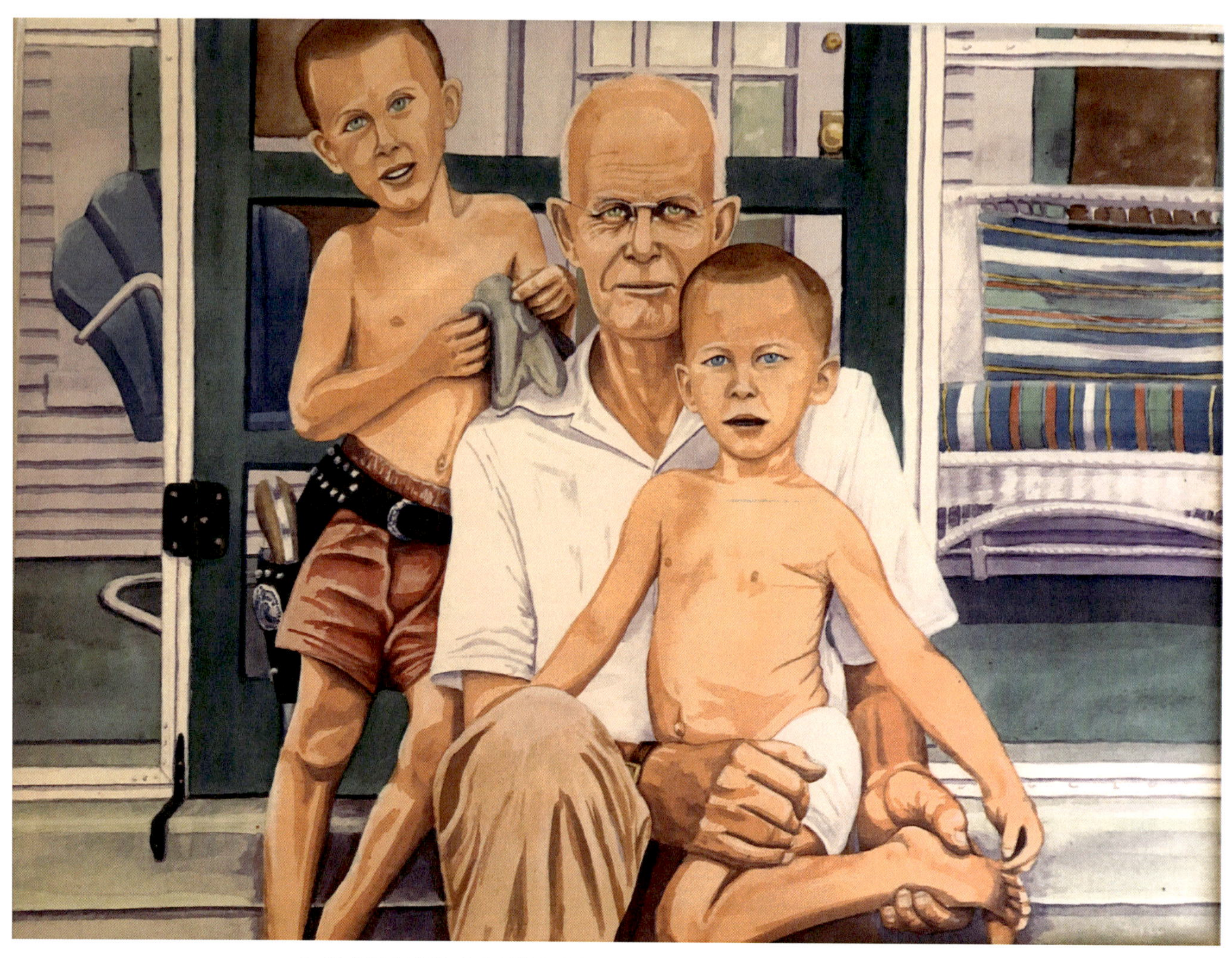

A MAN YOU COULD LEAN ON, 30X40, ACRYLIC*

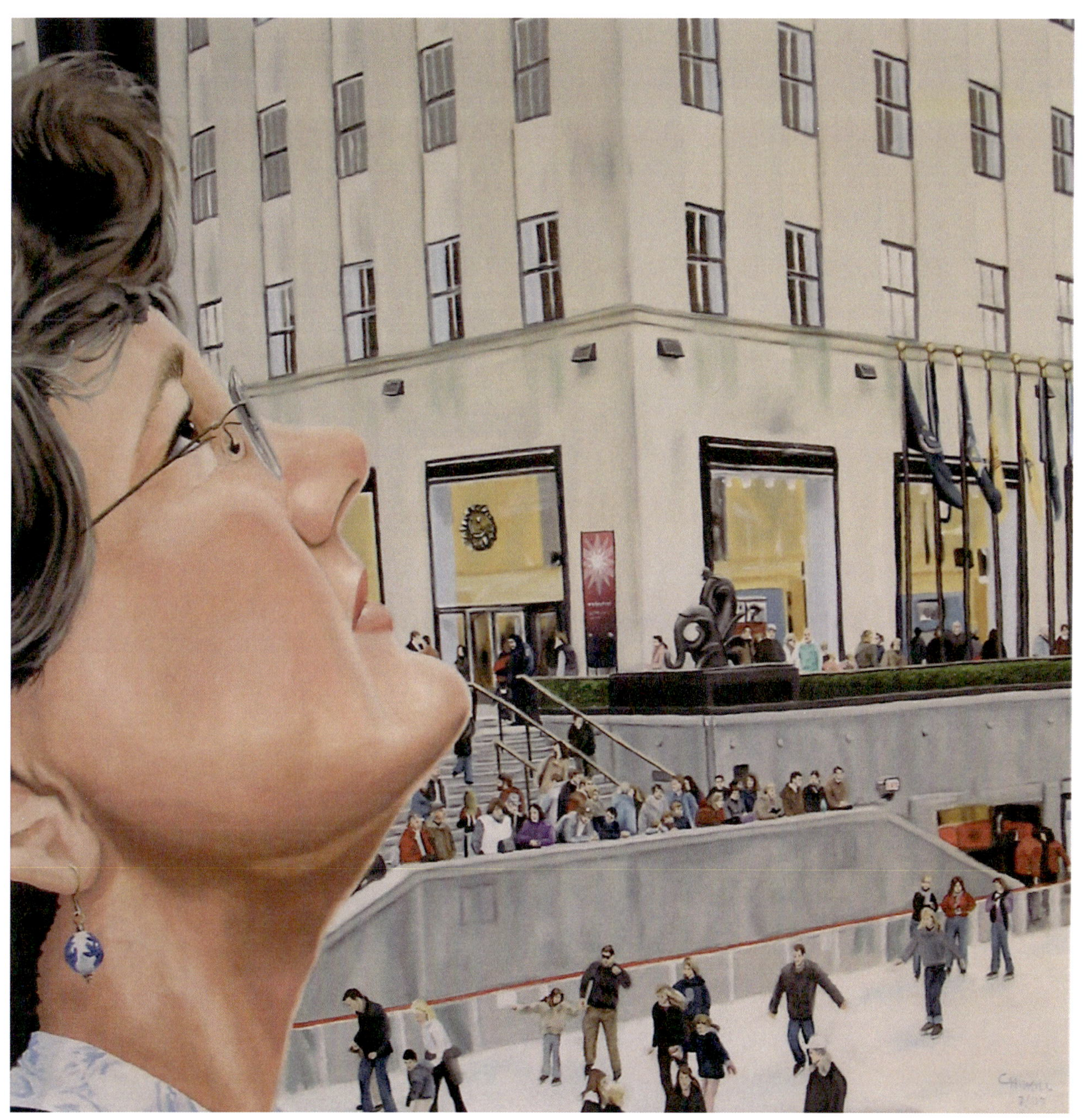

BET #7: ROCKEFELLER CENTER, 30X30*

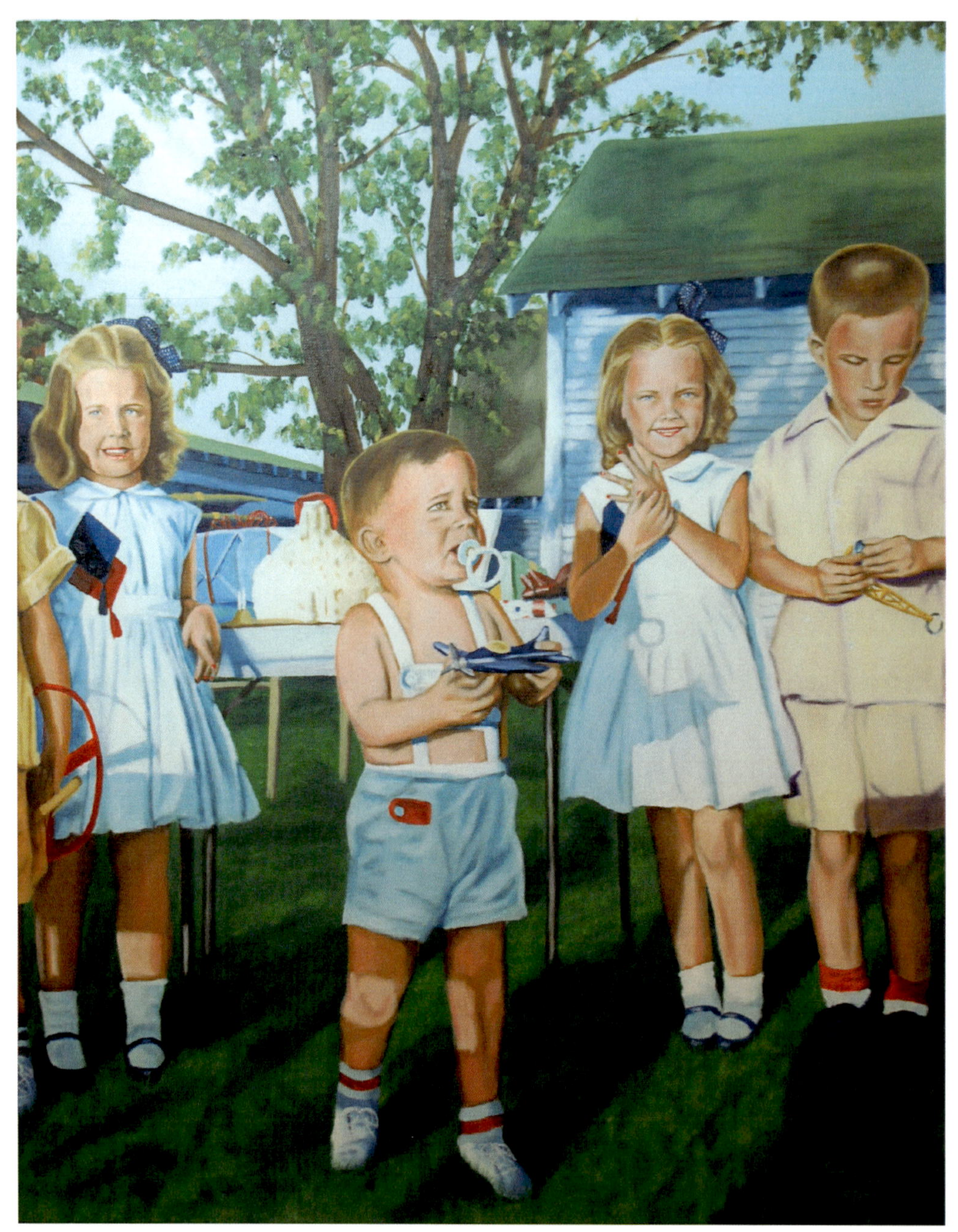

**BIRTHDAY PARTY, 24X30***

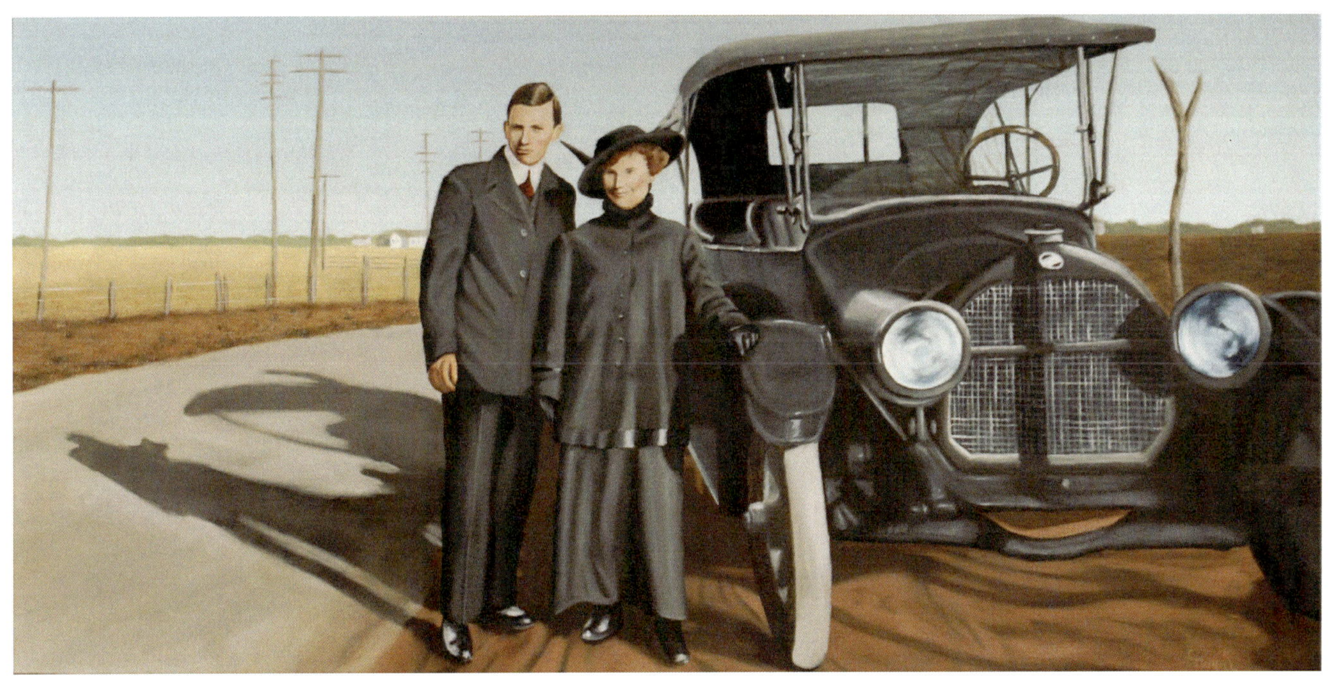

UNCLE LEWIS AND AUNT T, 24X48*

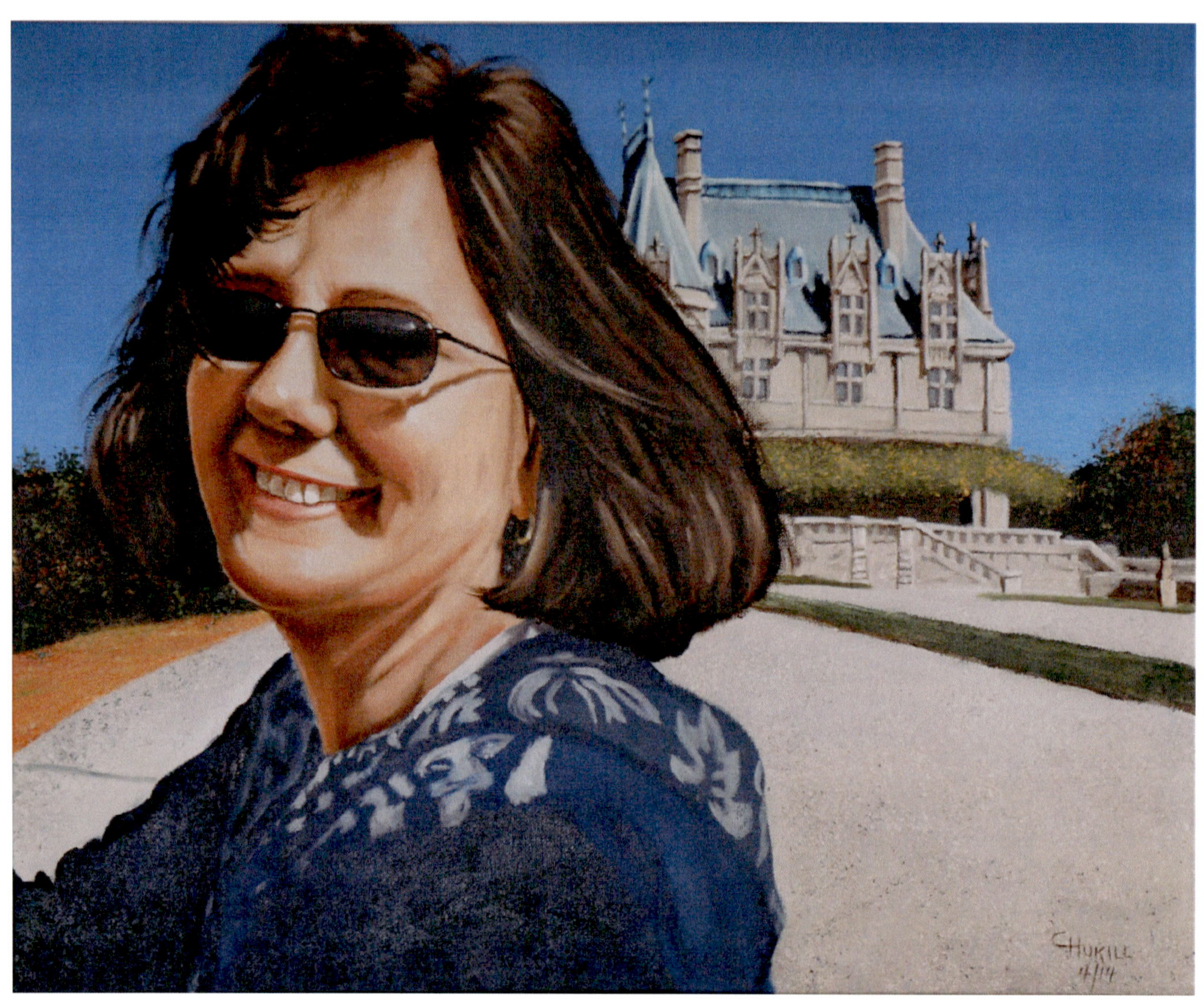

BET #11: BILTMORE, 16X20*

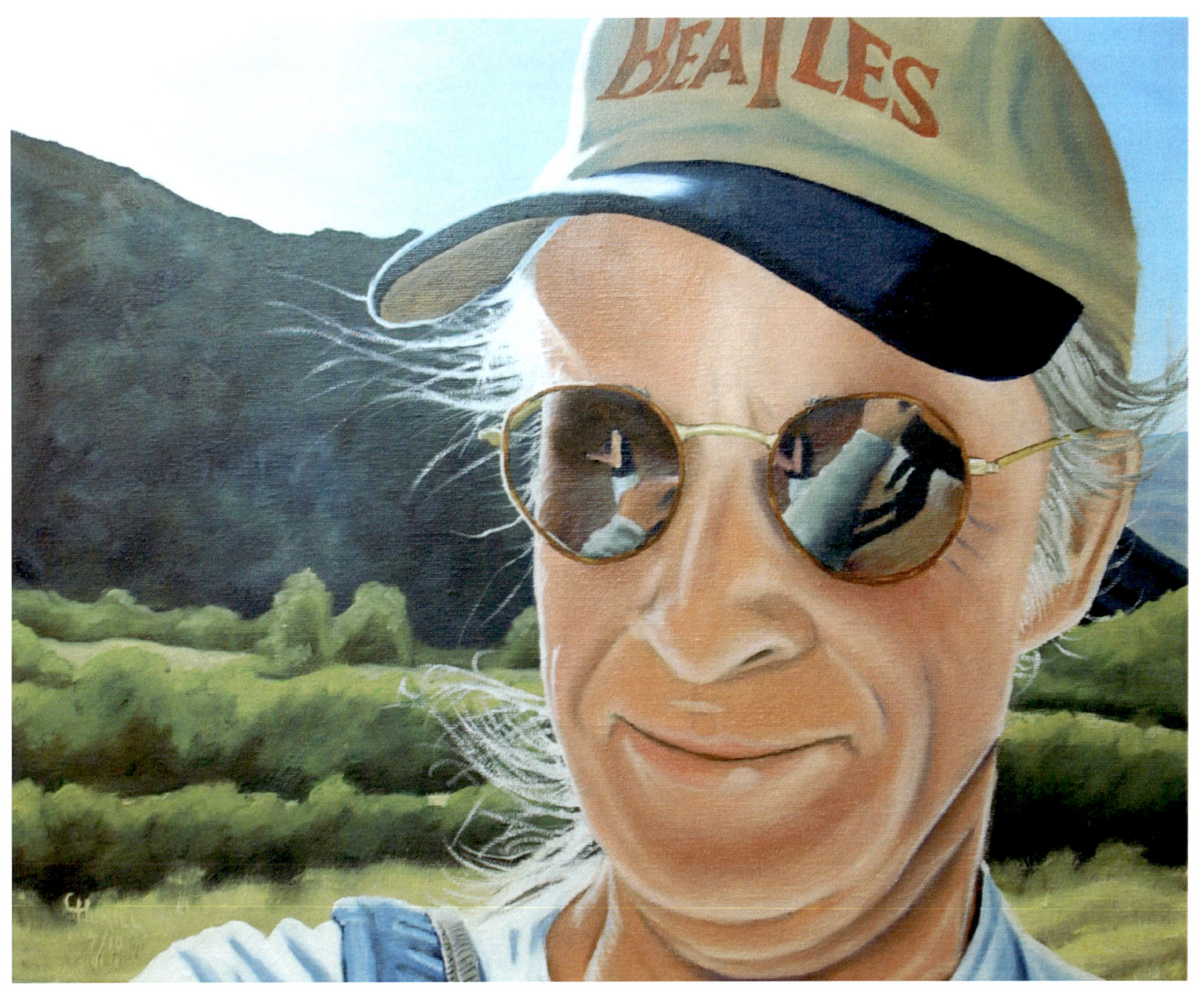


SELF-PORTRAIT AT THE WINDOW, 16X20*

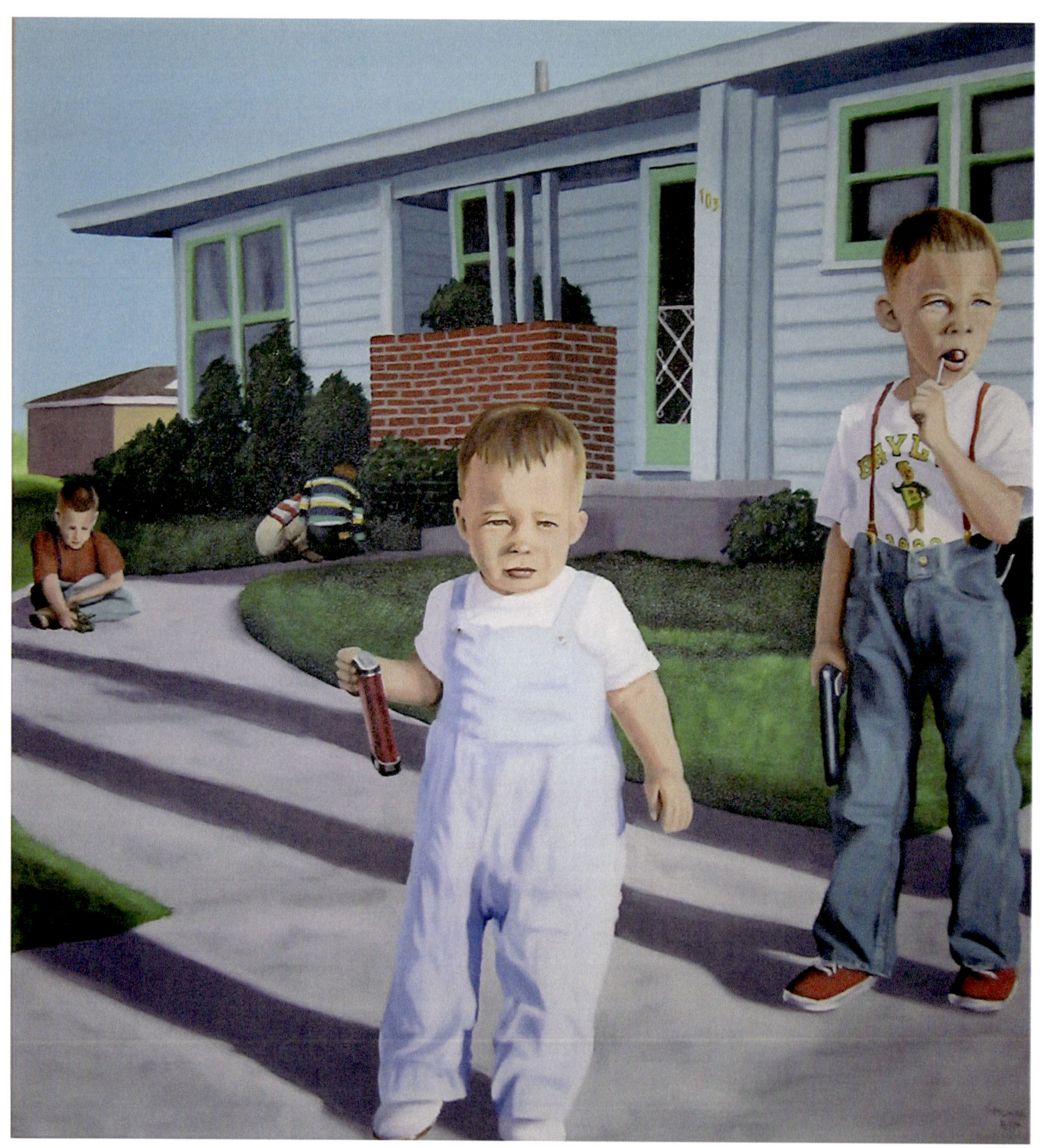

BROTHERS, 30X30*

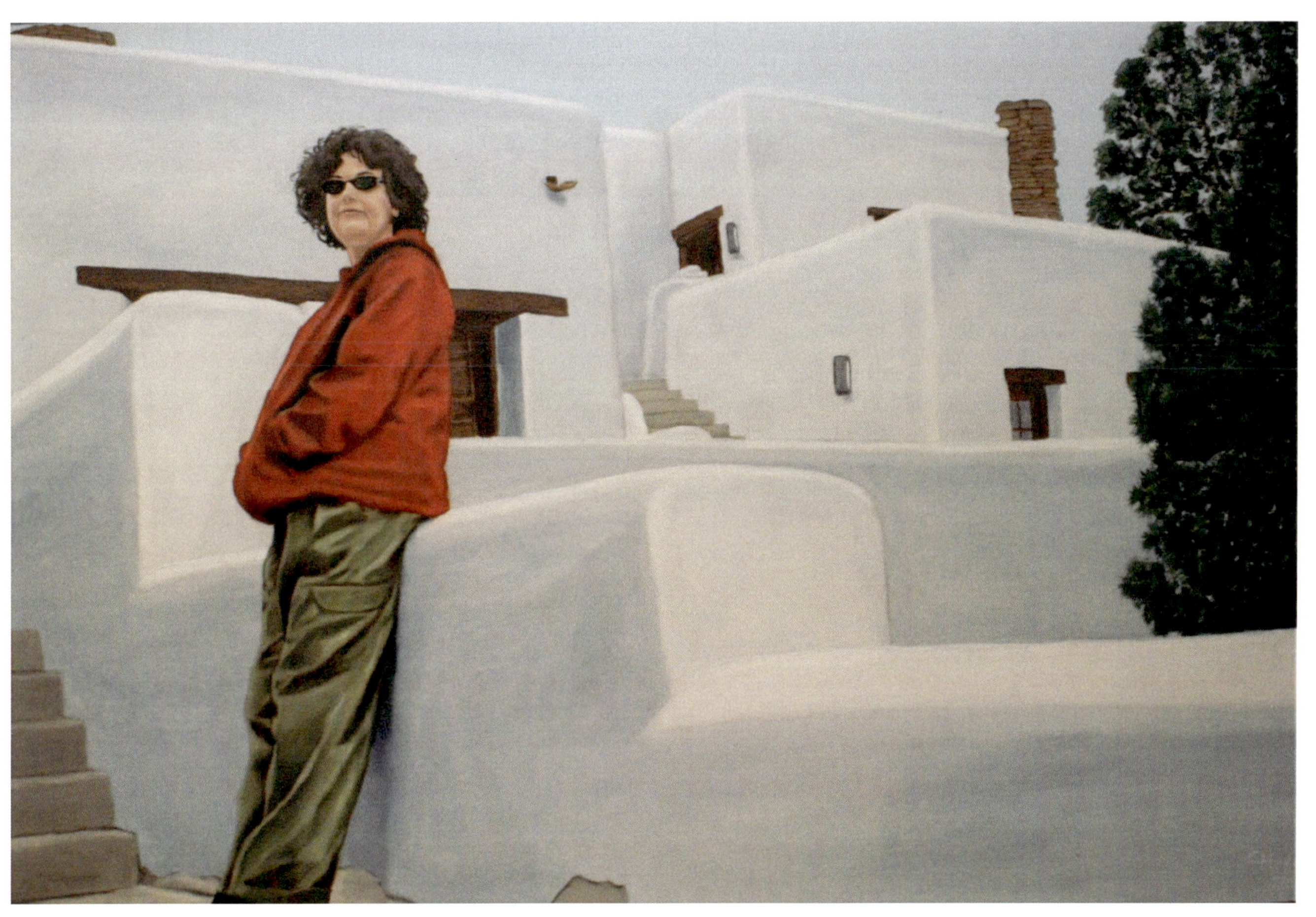

BET #8: INDIAN LODGE, 24X36*

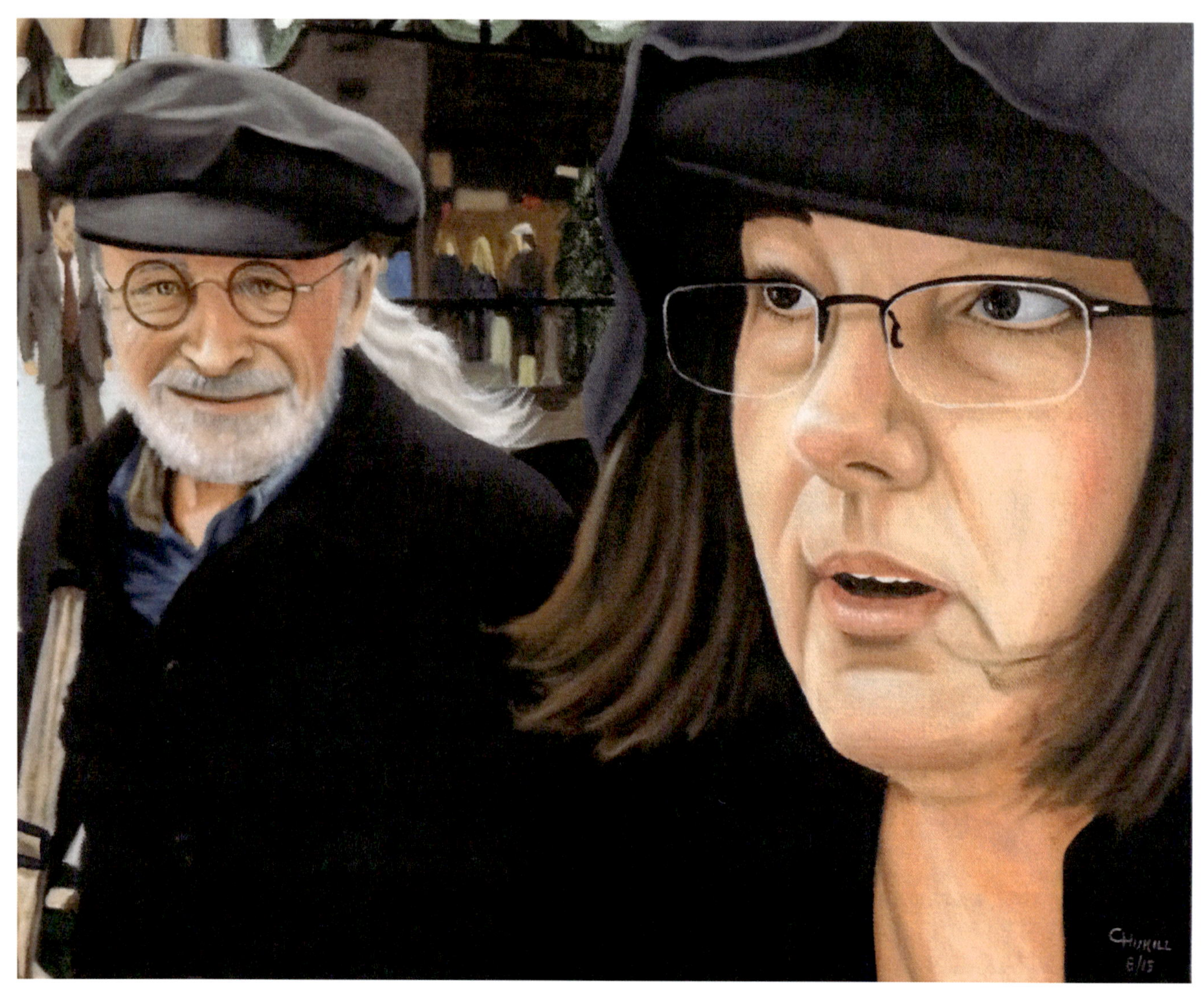

SELF-PORTRAIT WITH BET AT KEENLAND, 16X20*

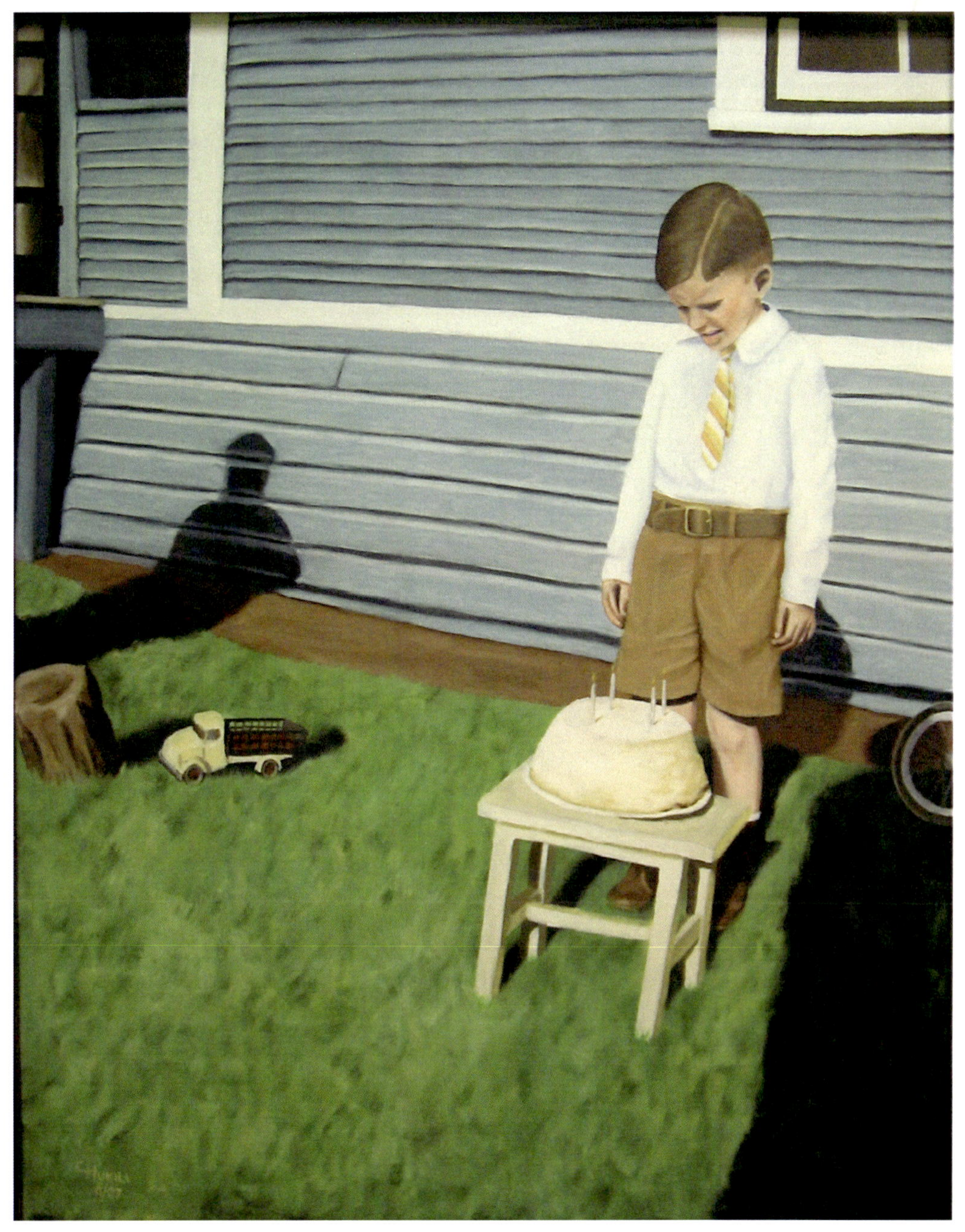

**HAPPY BIRTHDAY, 20X24***

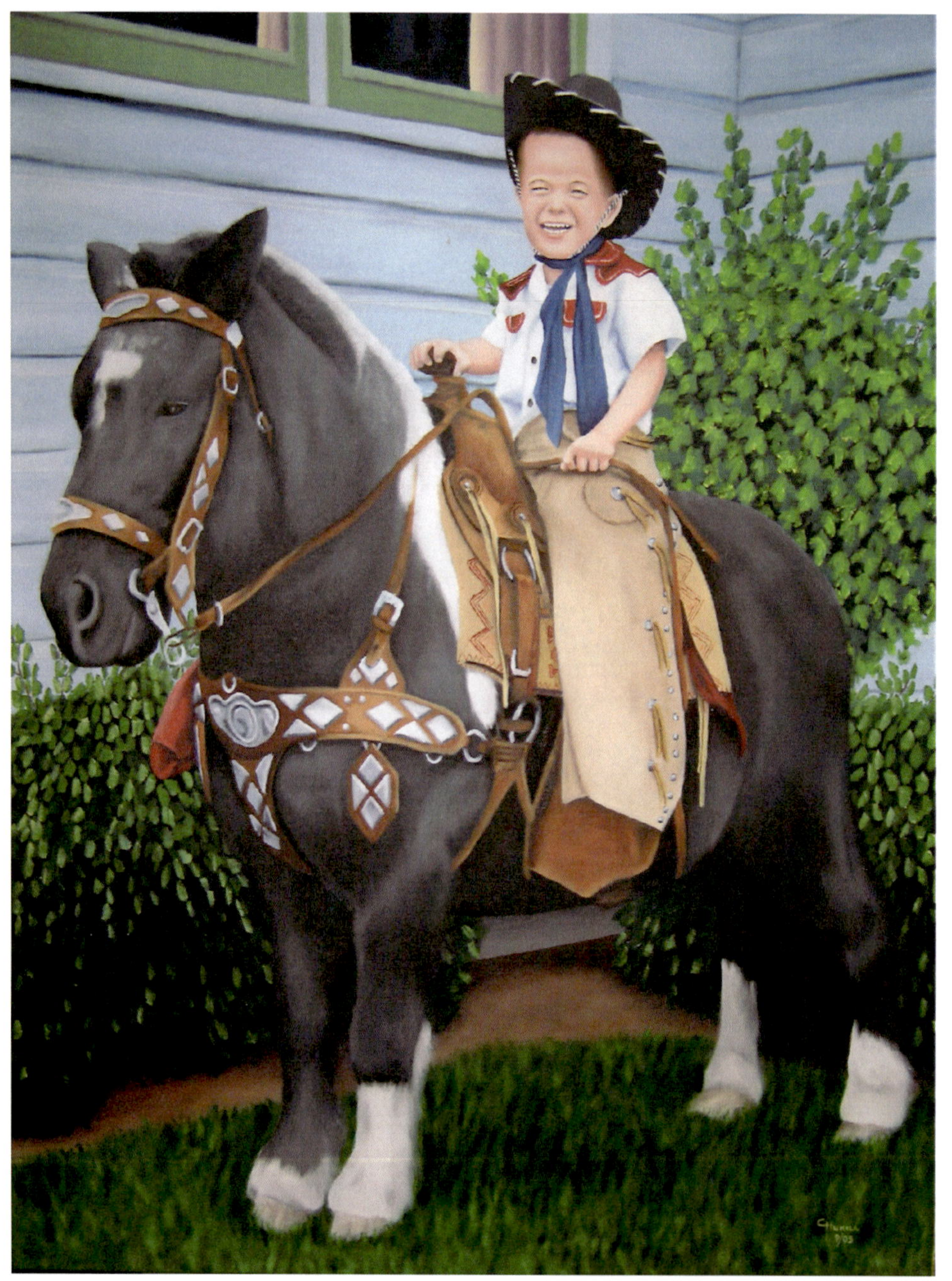

**PORTRAIT OF THE ARTIST AS A YOUNG COWBOY, 30X40***

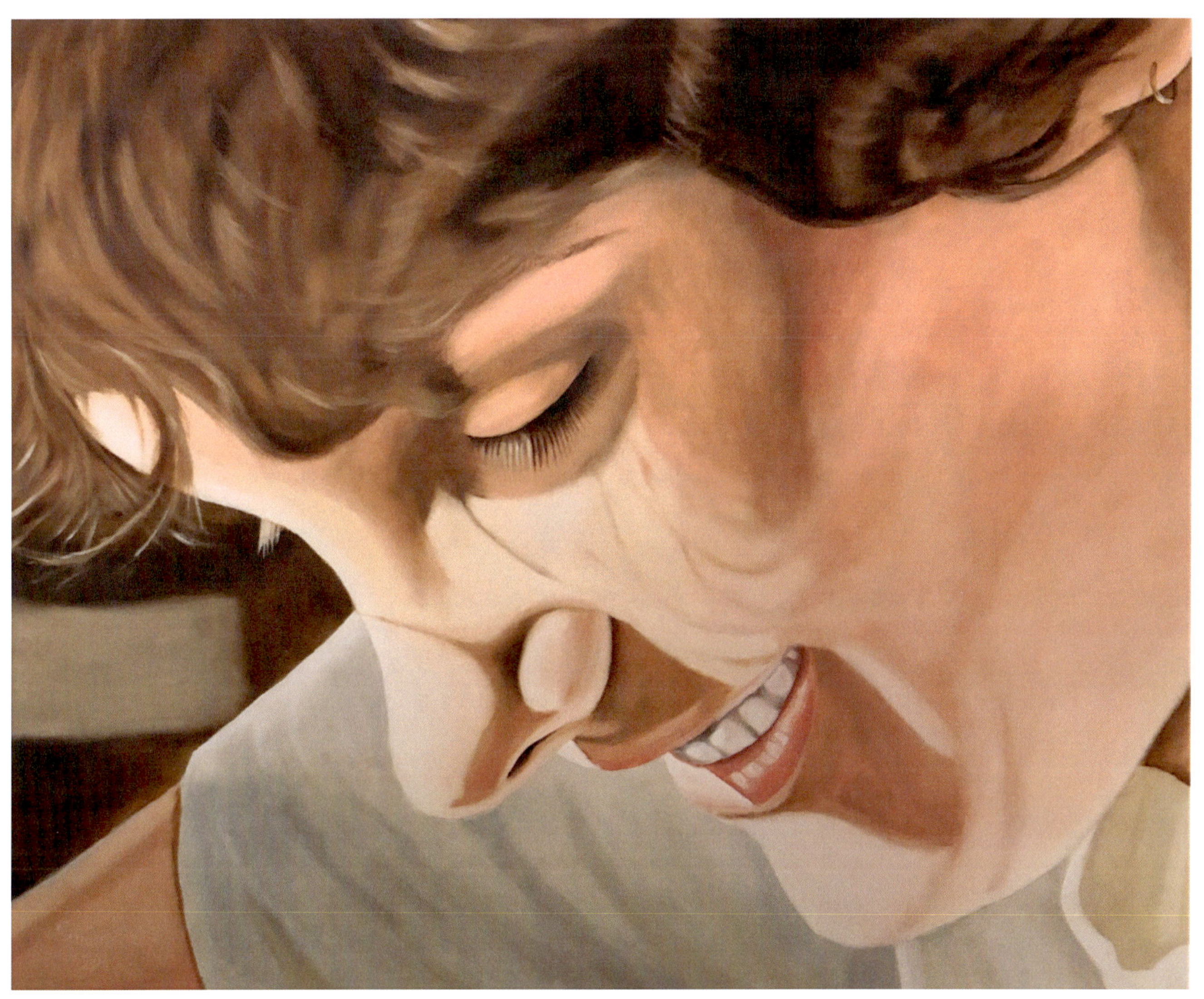

BET #5, 24X30*

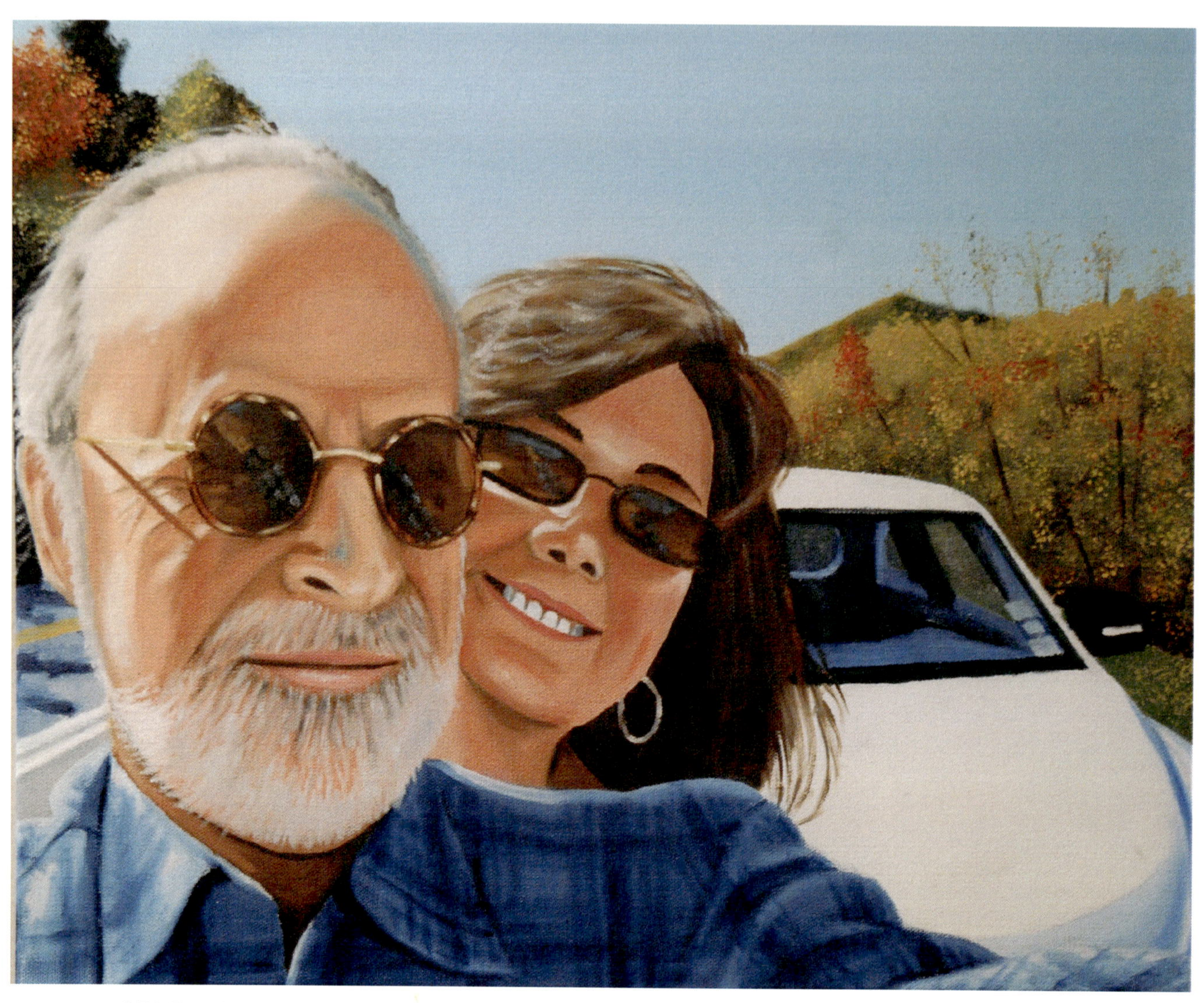

SELF-PORTRAIT WITH BET AND THE TURBO ON THE BLUE RIDGE, 16X20*

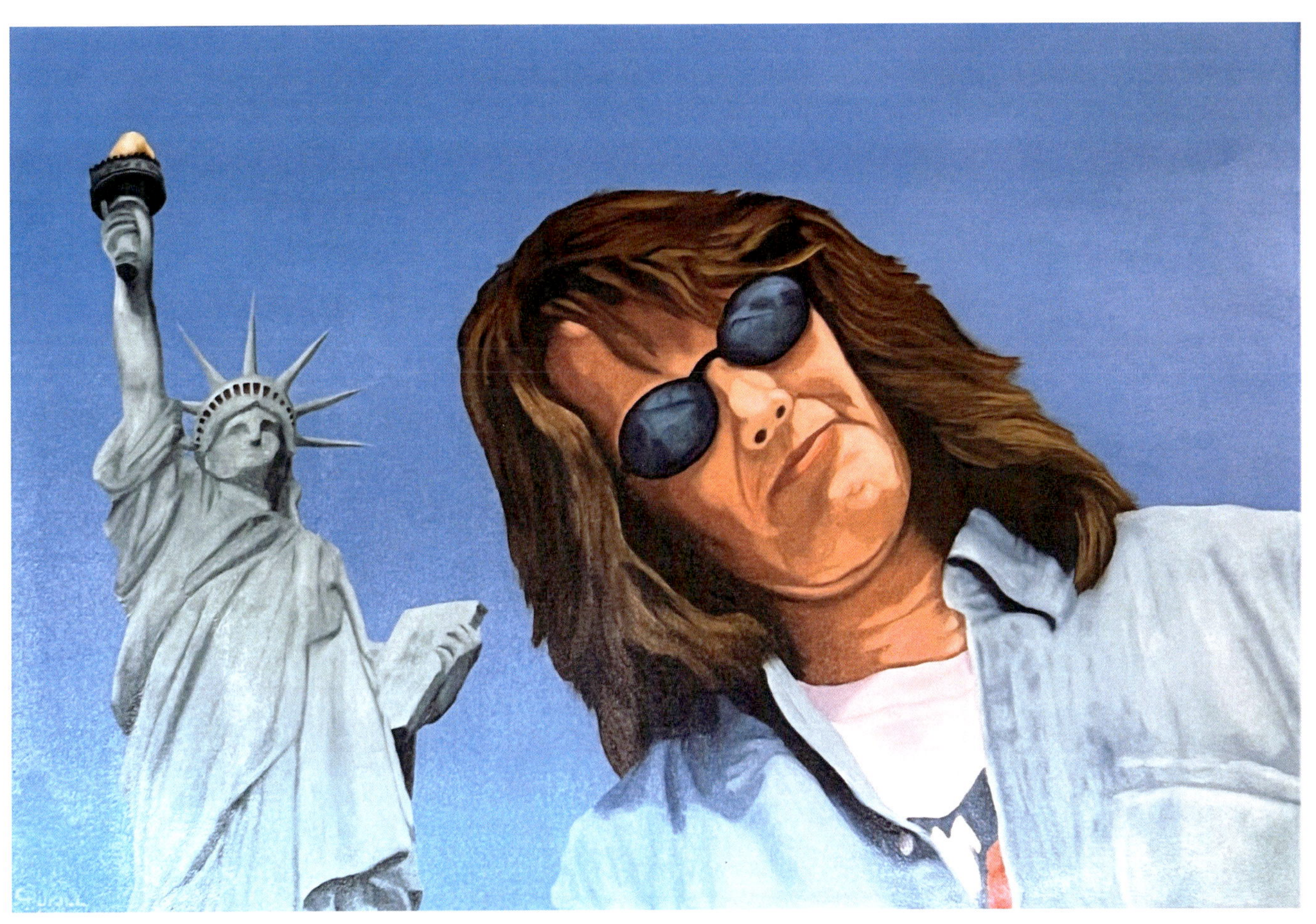

COUSIN SARA GETS LIBERATED, 20X24*

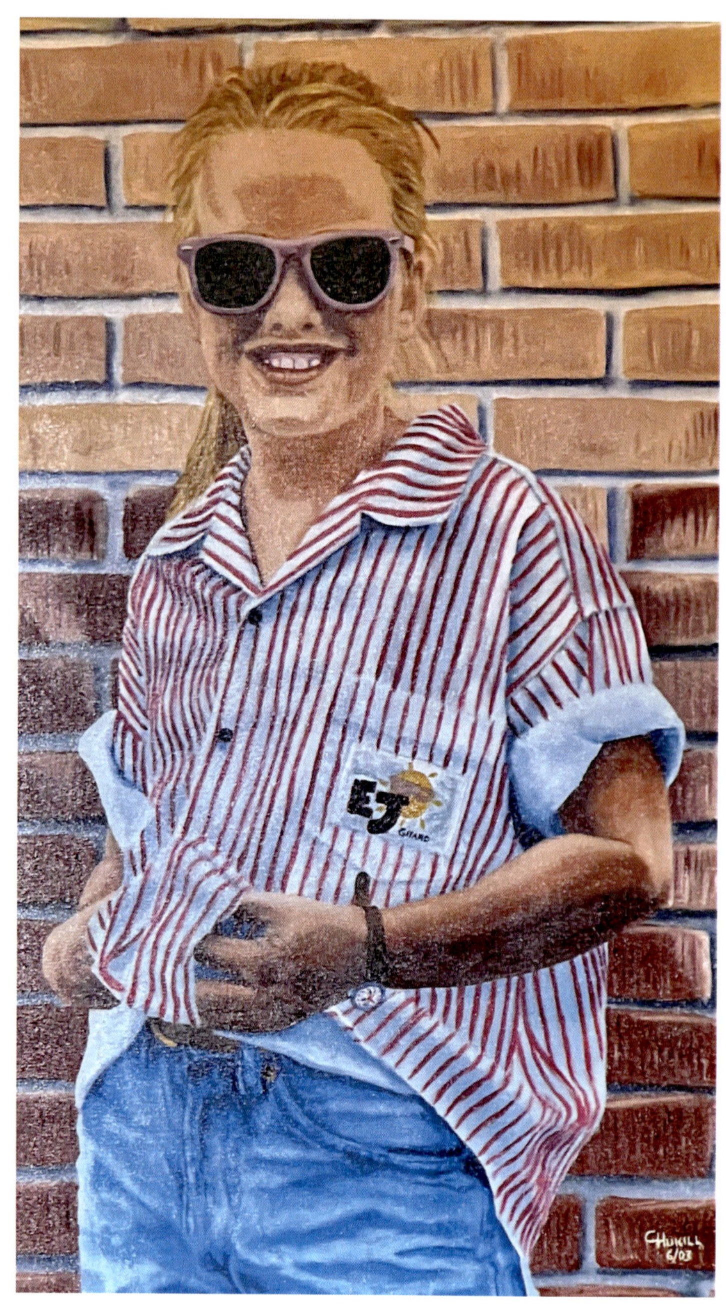

SHANNON, THE COOL, 24X30*

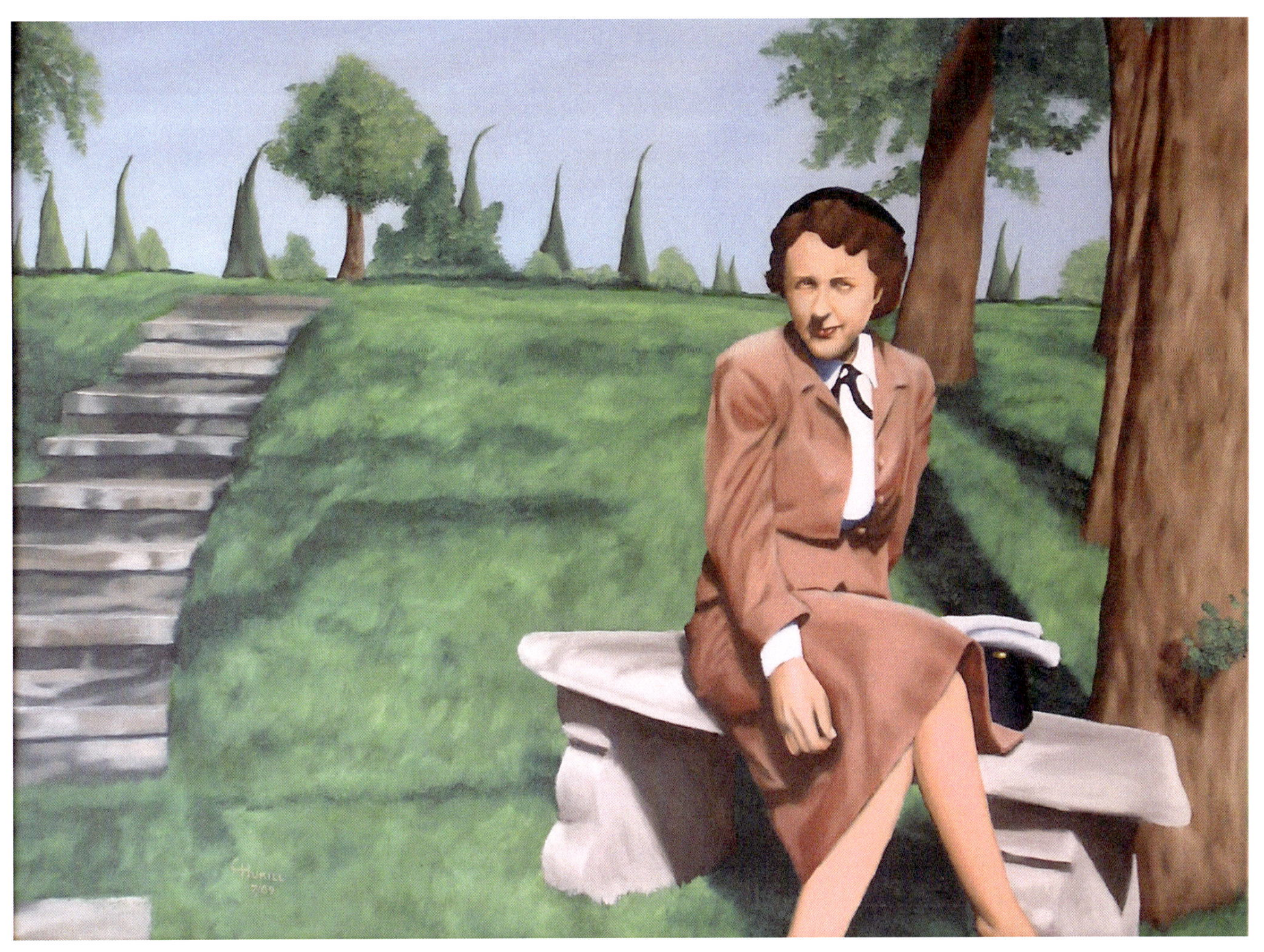

VIRGINIA, 24X30*

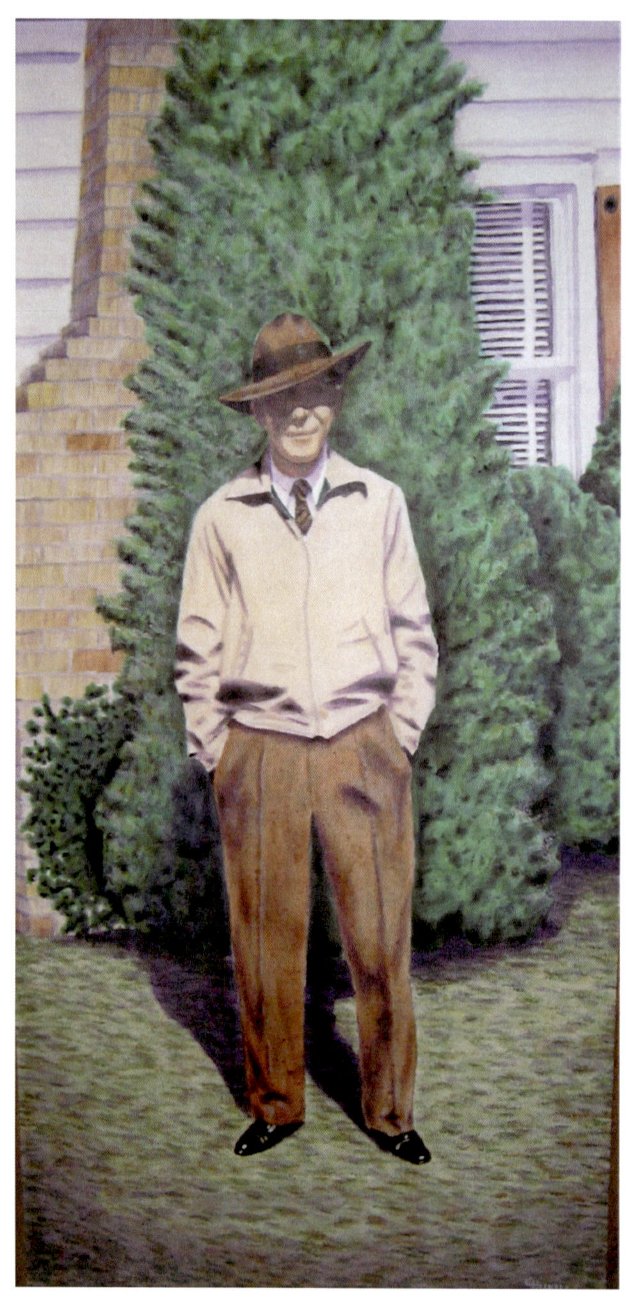

**MAN, 24X48, ACRYLIC***

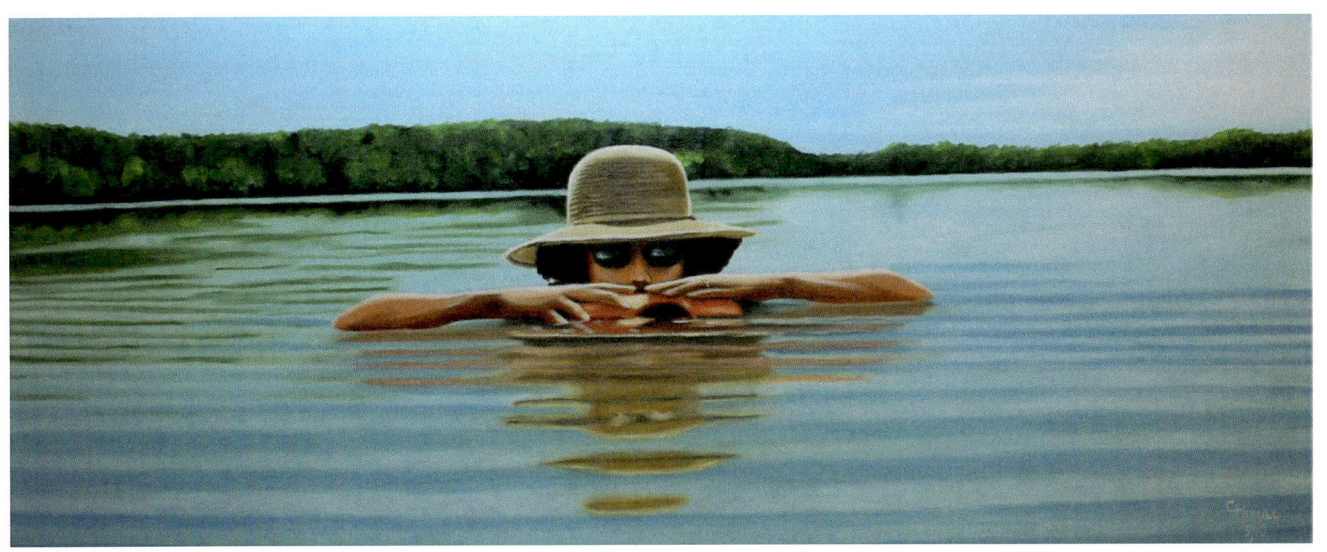

BET #10: CLEBURNE STATE PARK, 16X40*

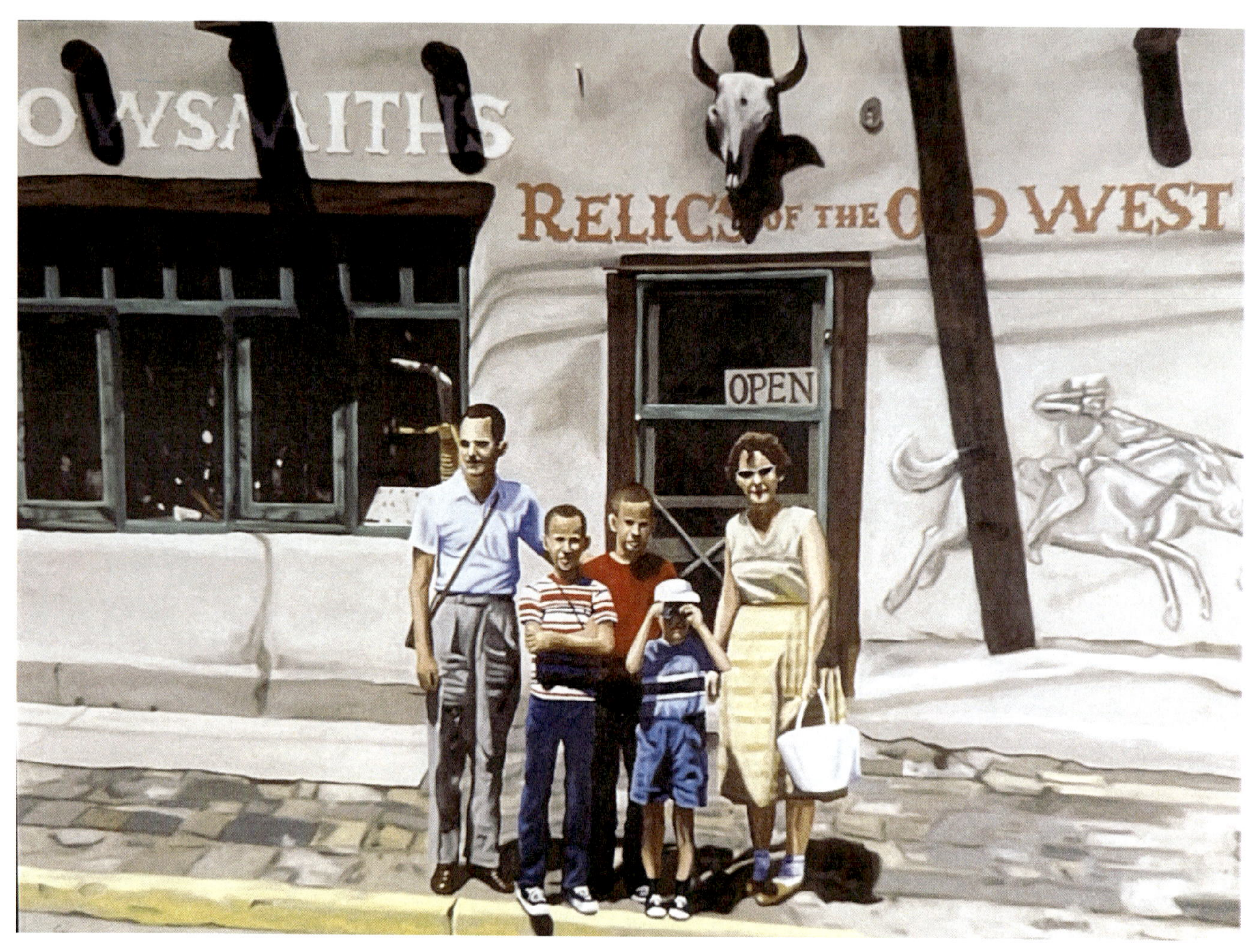


THE NUCLEAR FAMILY: RELICS OF THE OLD WEST, 30X40*

# We Are What We Drive

These images are from a 2013 Center for Contemporary Arts show, "Fenders and Headlights". Americans have long had a love affair with the automobile and this romance has played a significant role in defining who we are. I was struck by how often we photograph ourselves with our cars.

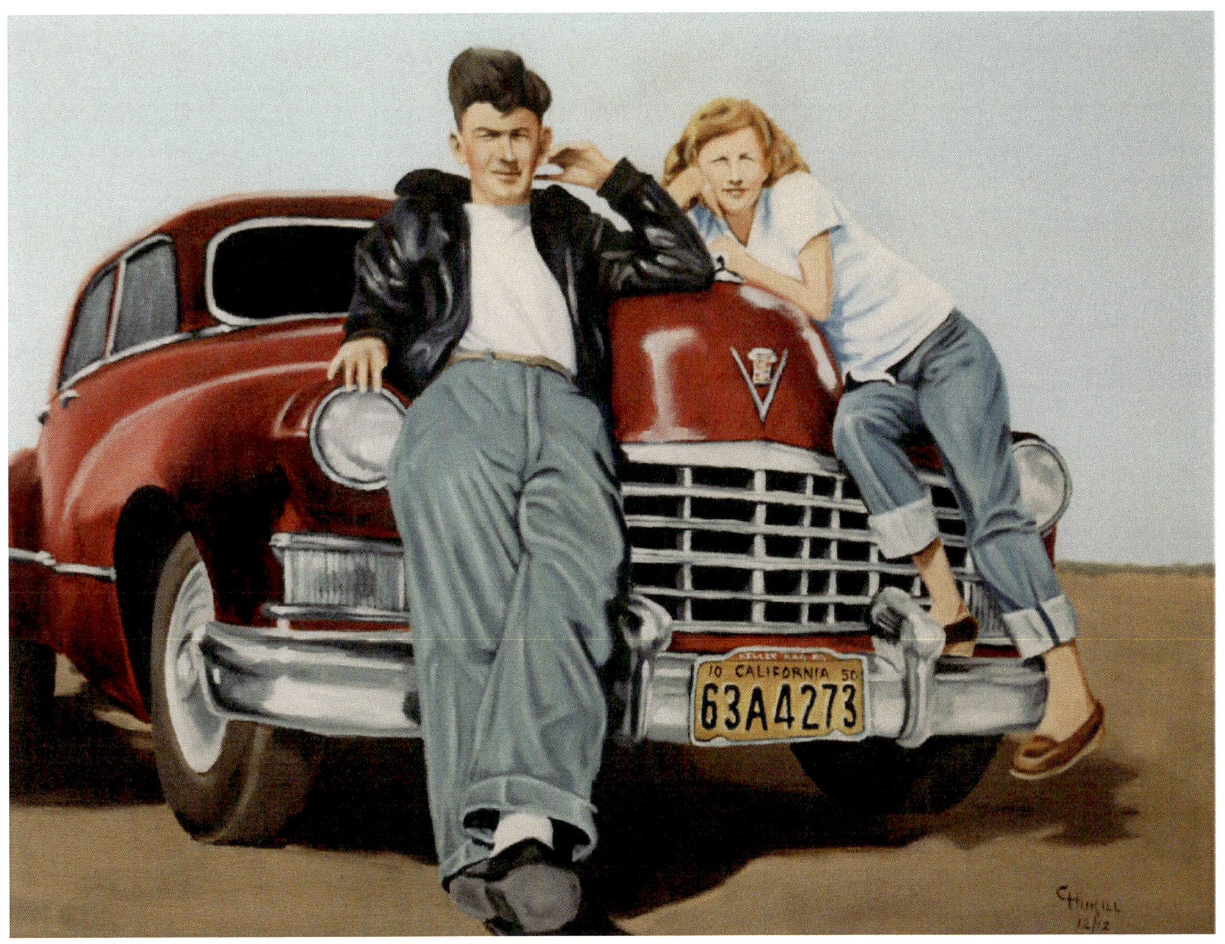

**ROCKABILLY DREAMERS, 18X24***

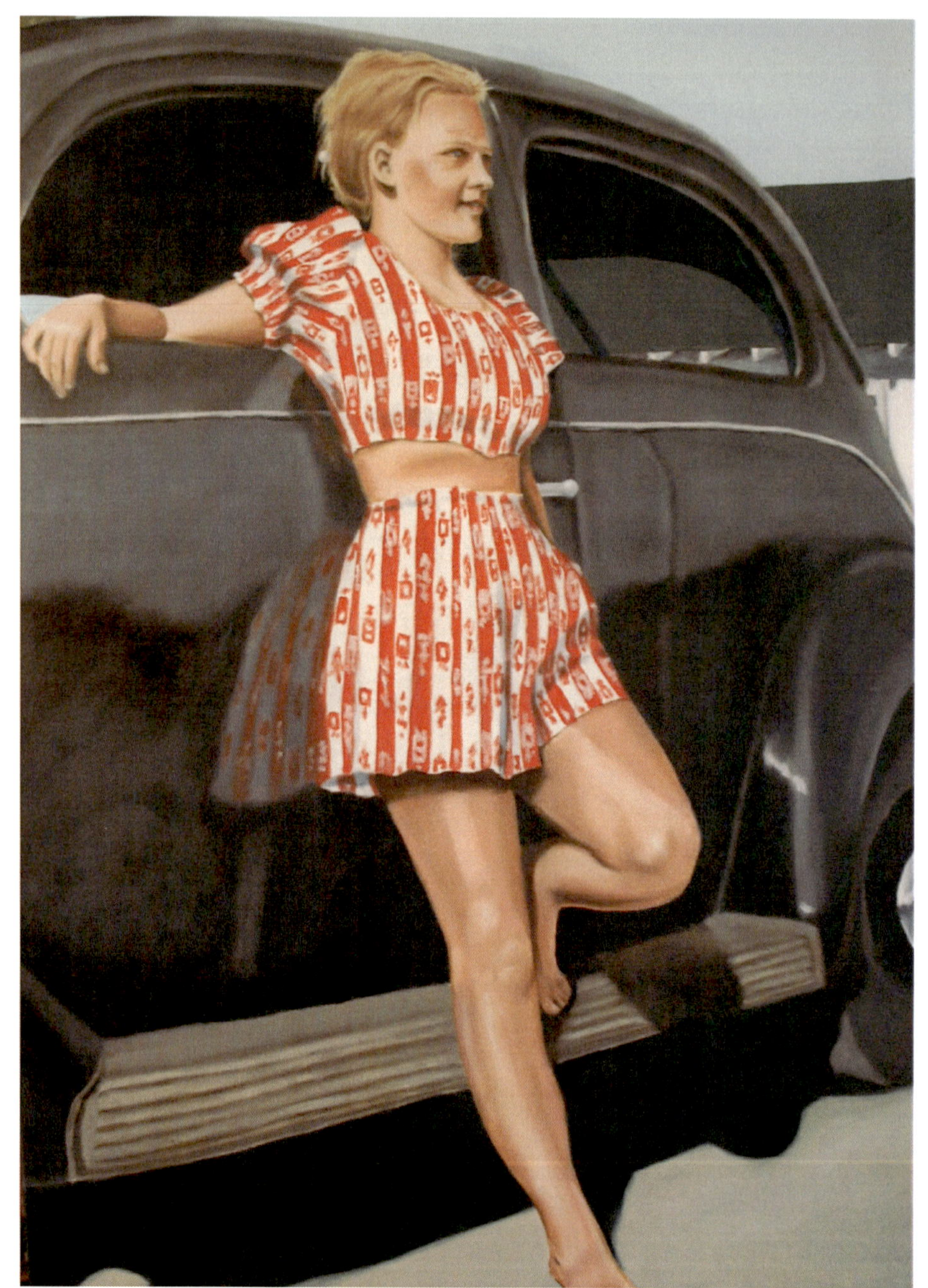

FENDERS AND HEADLIGHTS #2, 24X36*

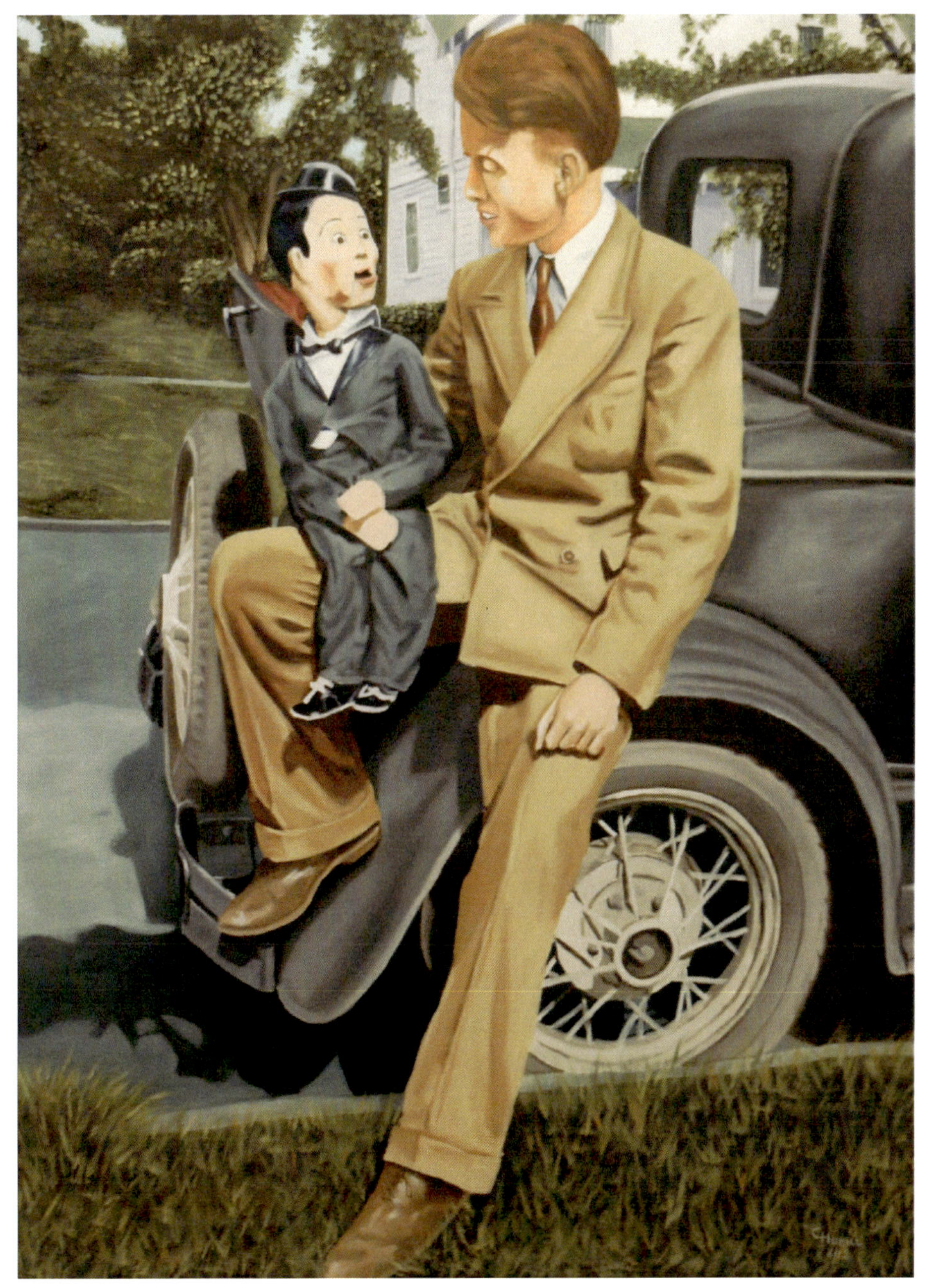

"NO, YOU CAN'T DRIVE," 30X40

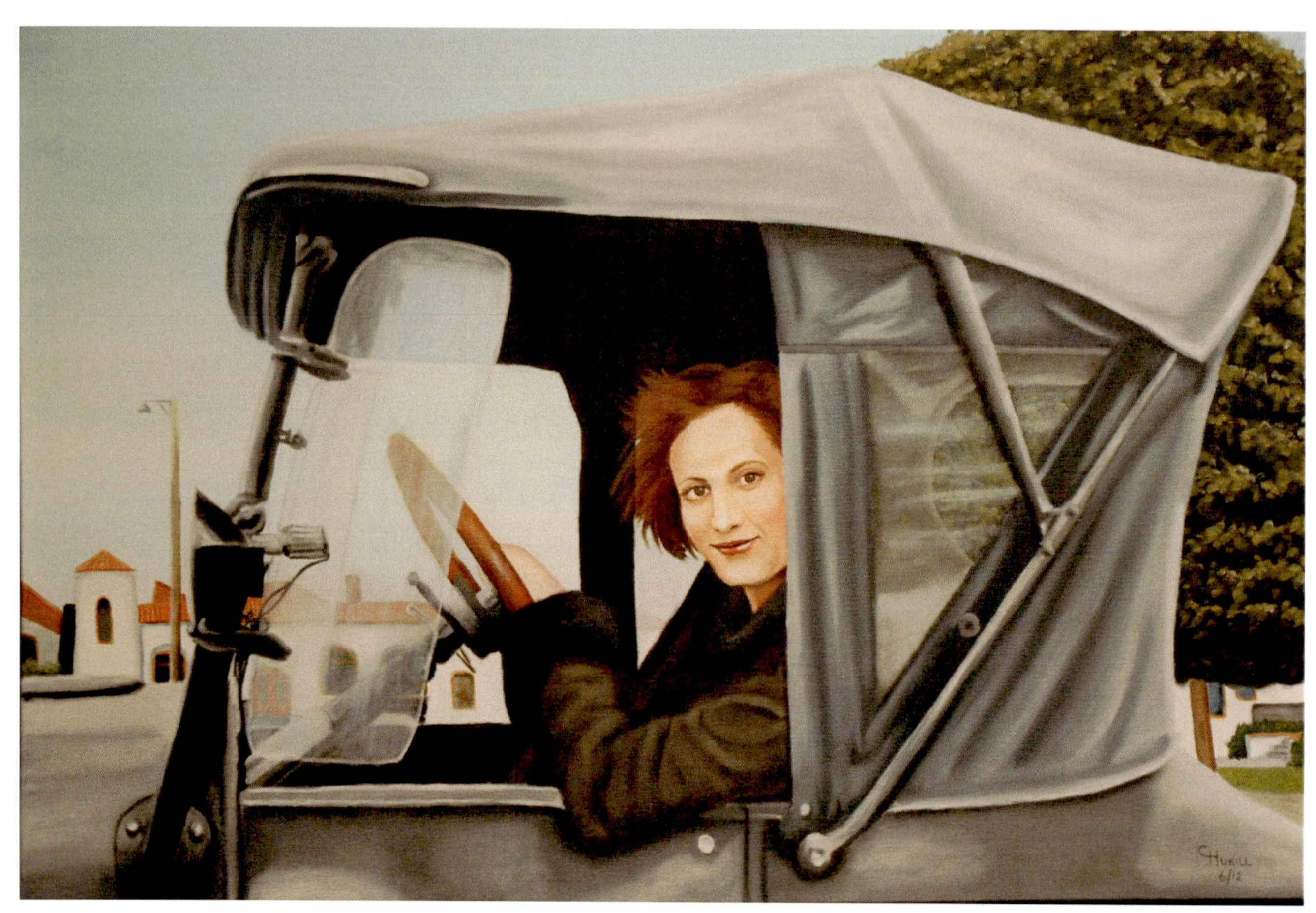

FLAPPER IN A FLIVVER, 24X30

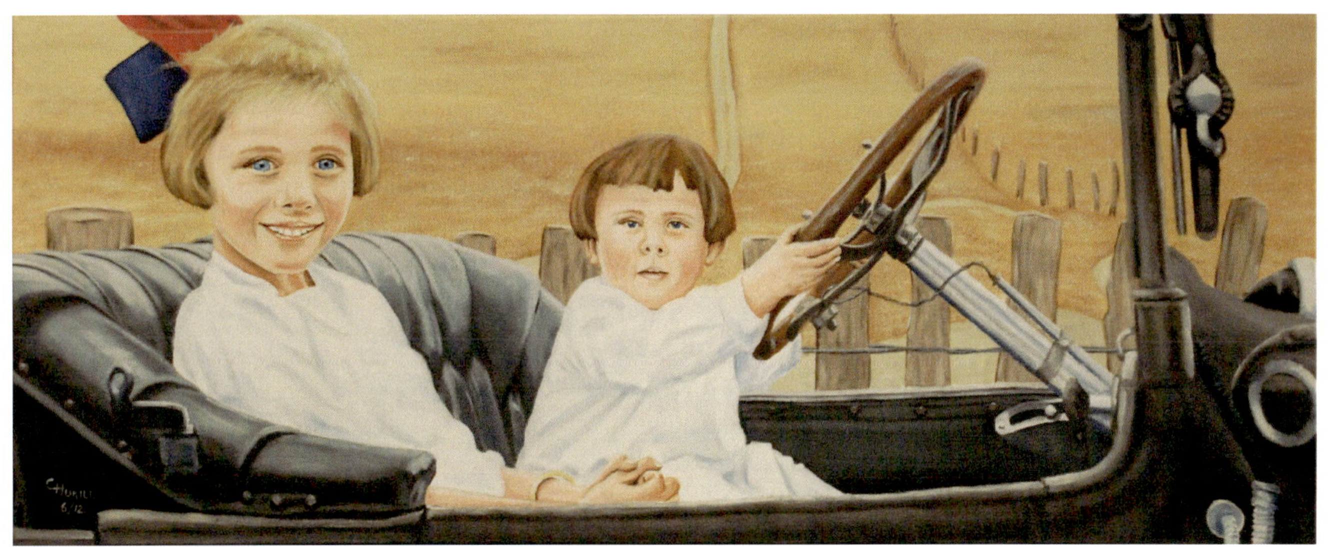

DRIVER EDUCATION, 16X40

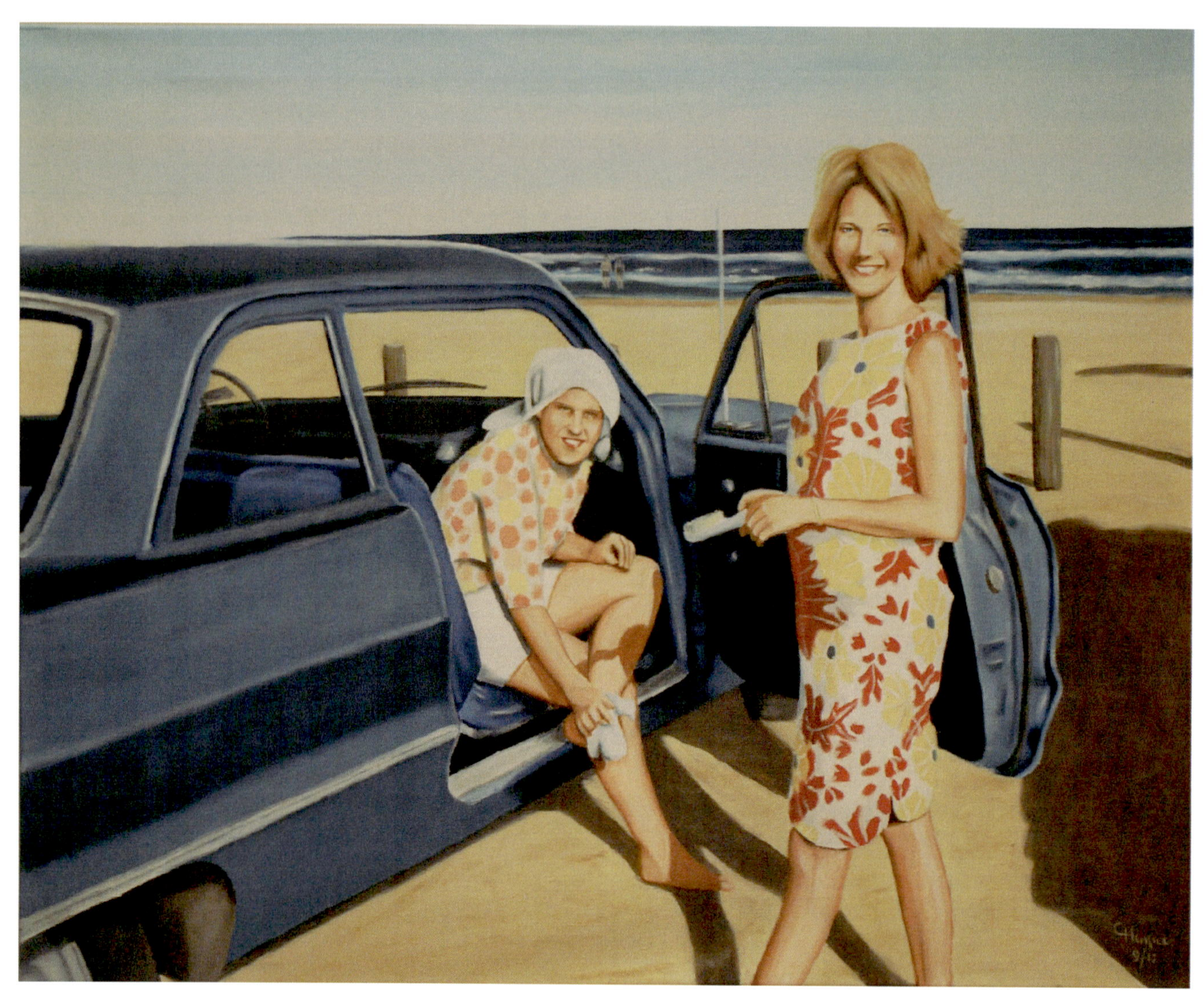

AT THE BEACH WITH KAREN AND BARBARA, 24X30*

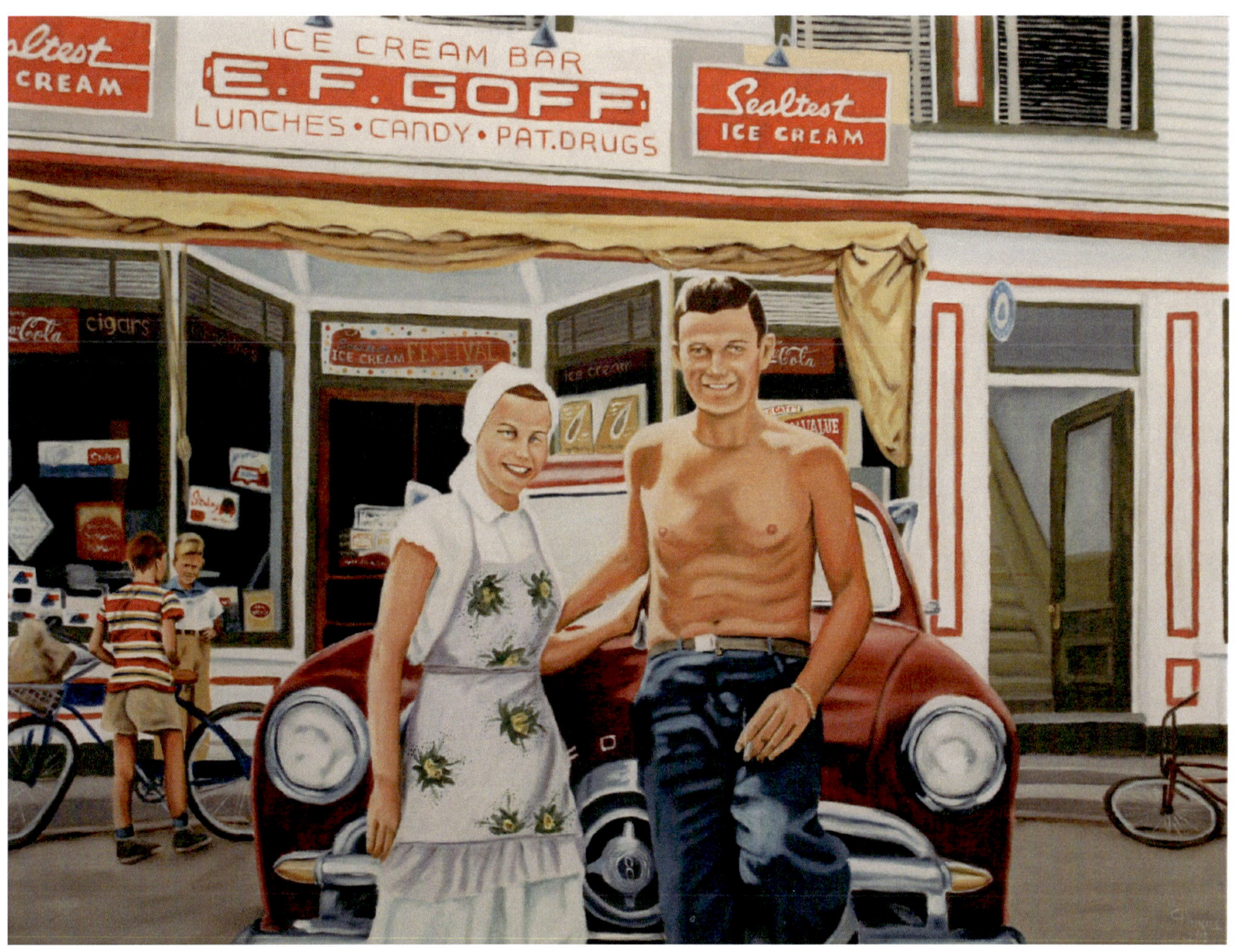



SEALTEST, 30X40

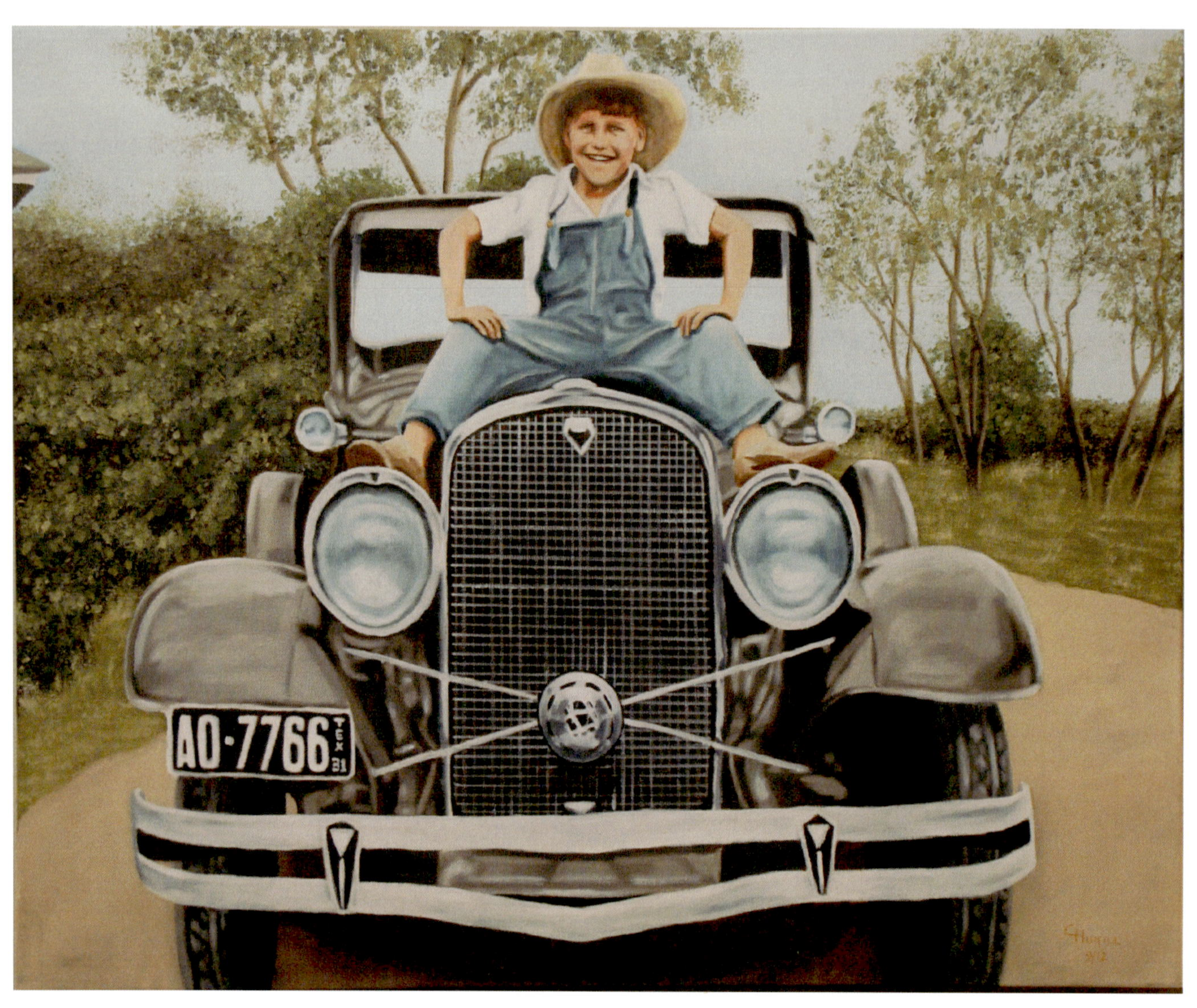

JOHN ALLEN RIDES AGAIN, 24X30*

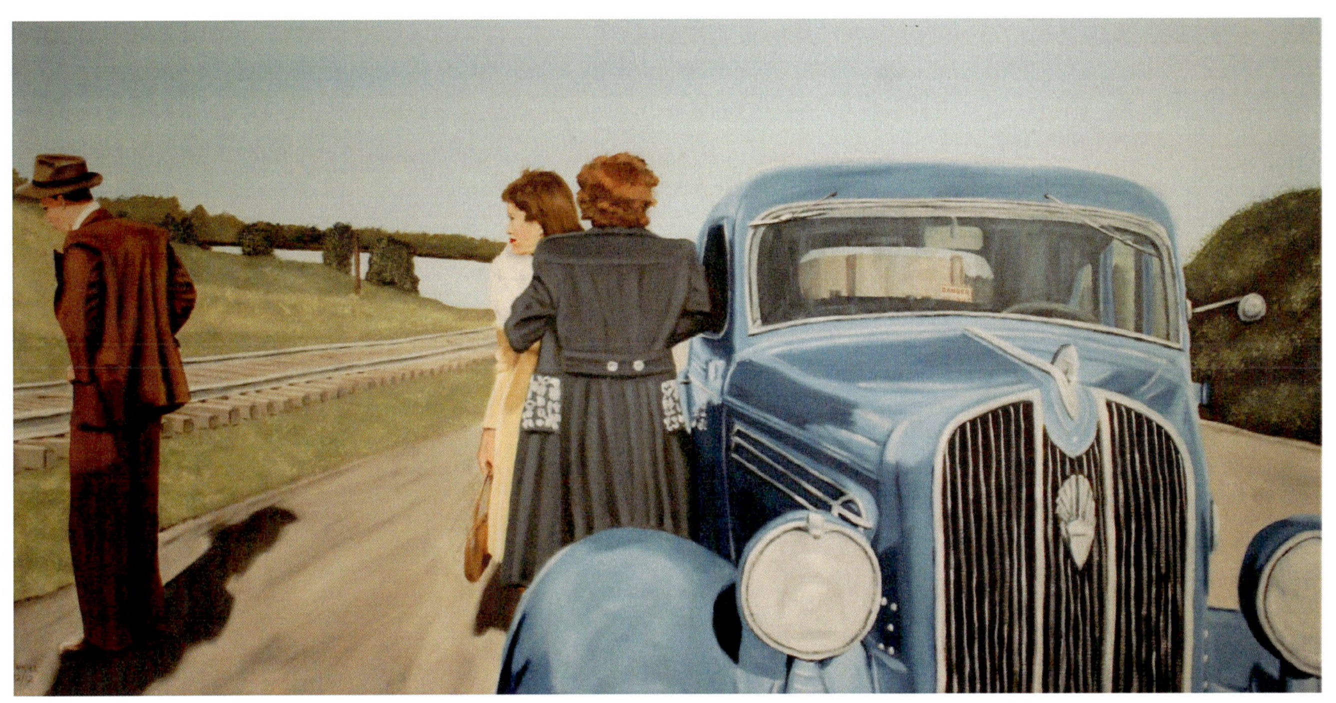

DANGER, 24X48

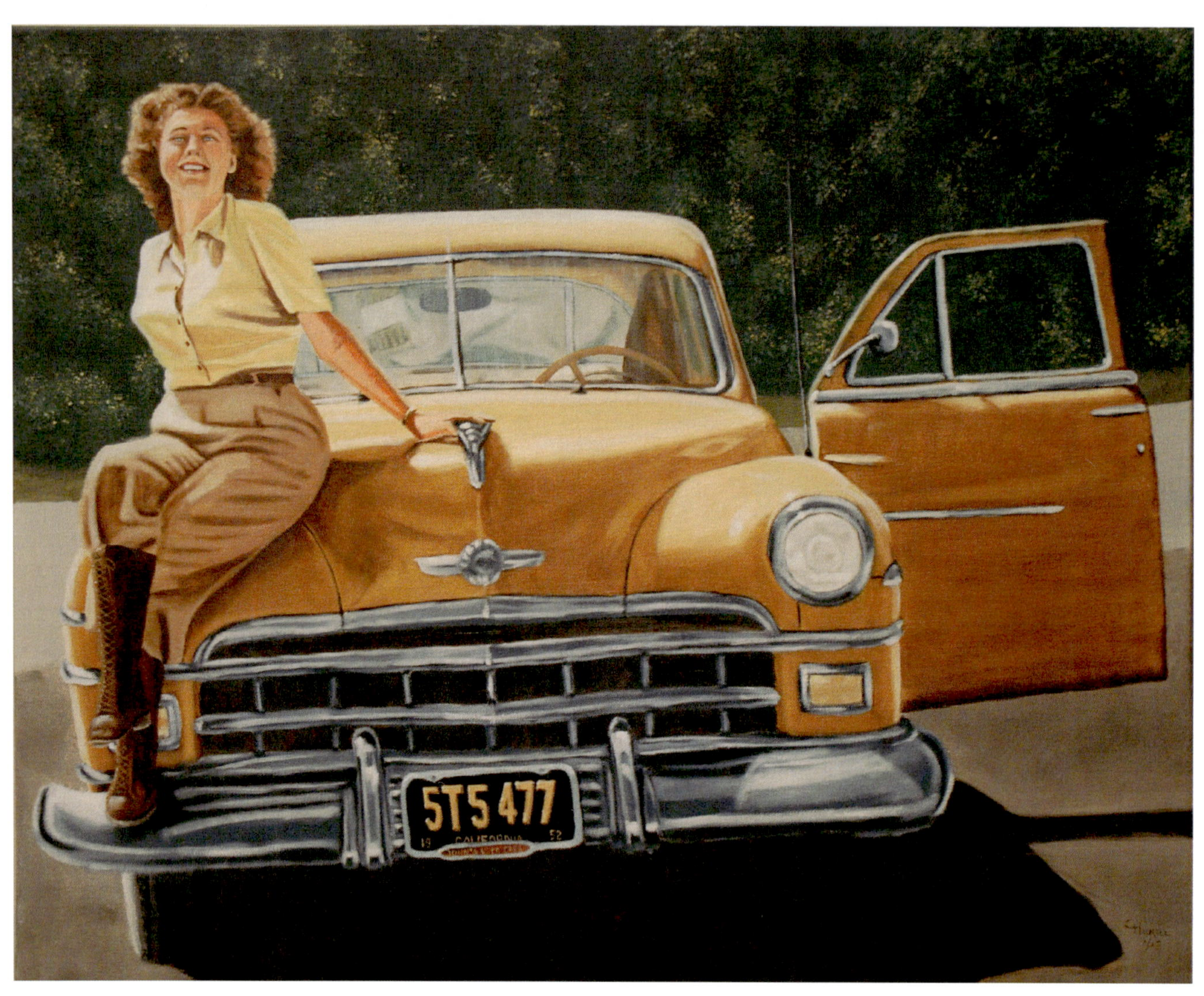

FENDERS AND HEADLIGHTS #6, 24X30*

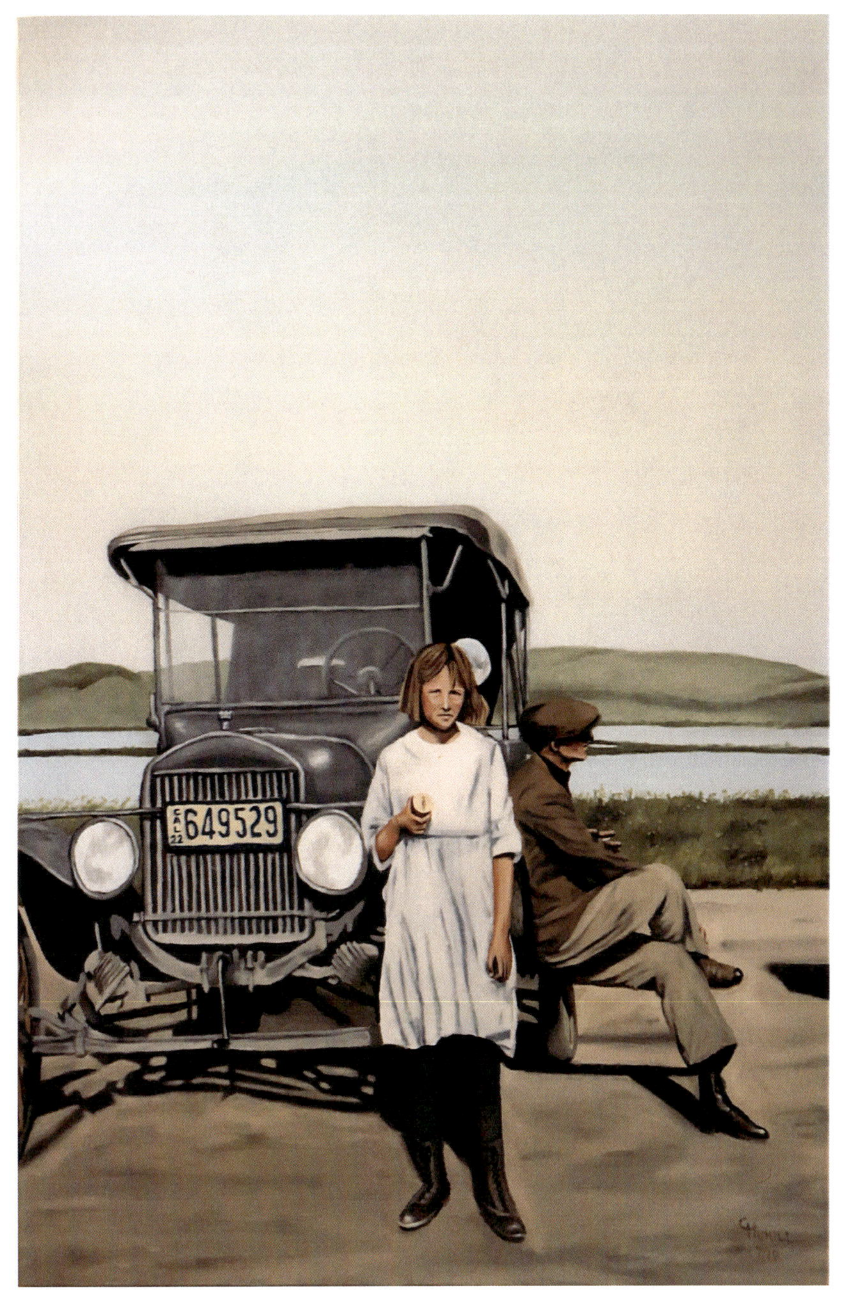


AN APPLE A DAY..., 24X36

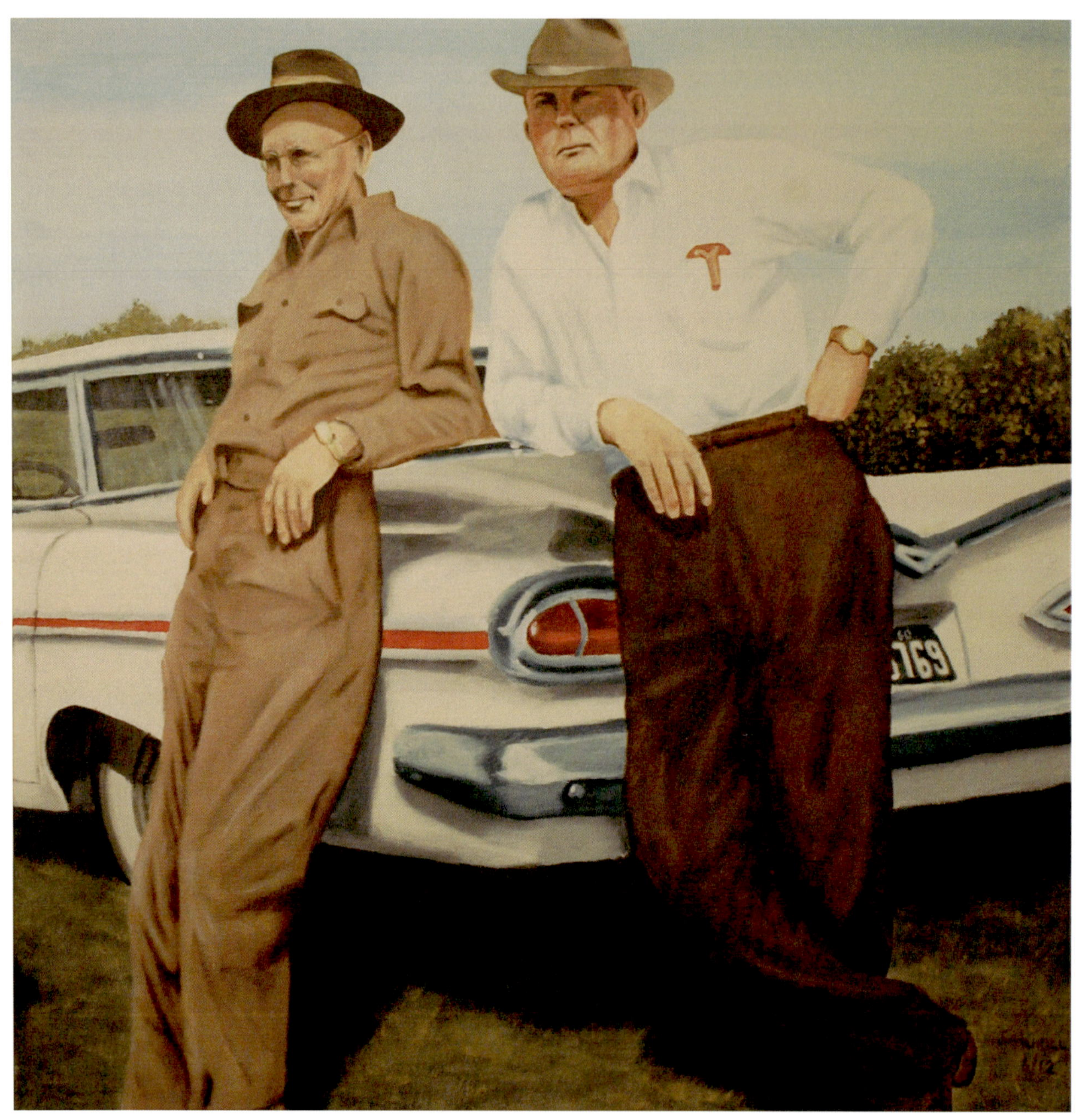

**REDNECKS AND TAILFINS, 24X24***

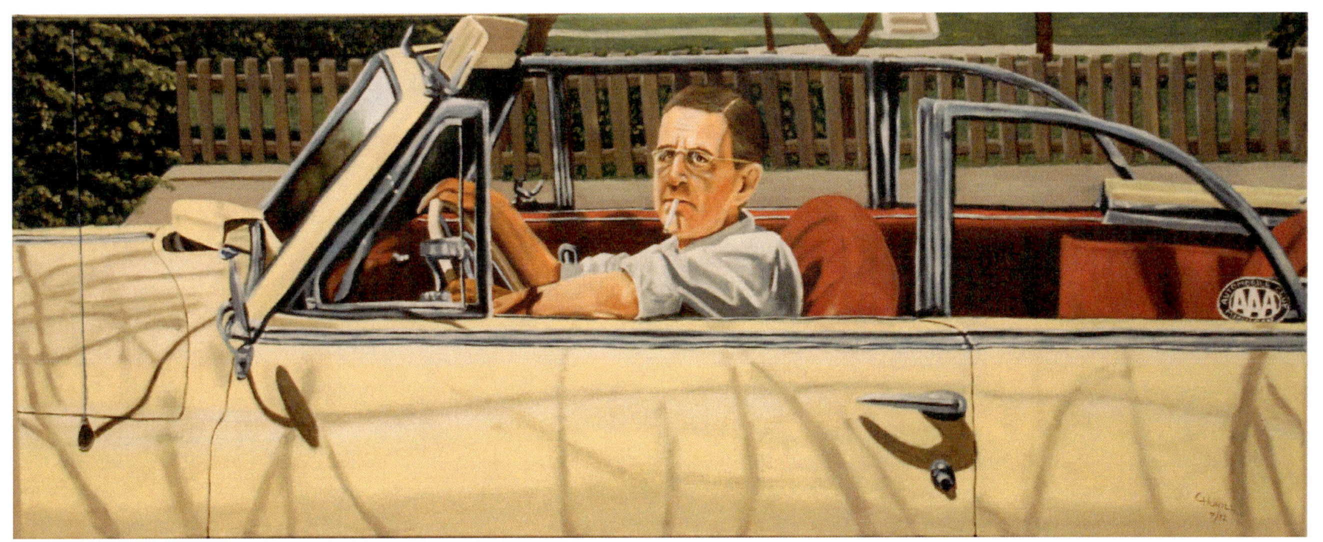

TRIPLE A, 16X40

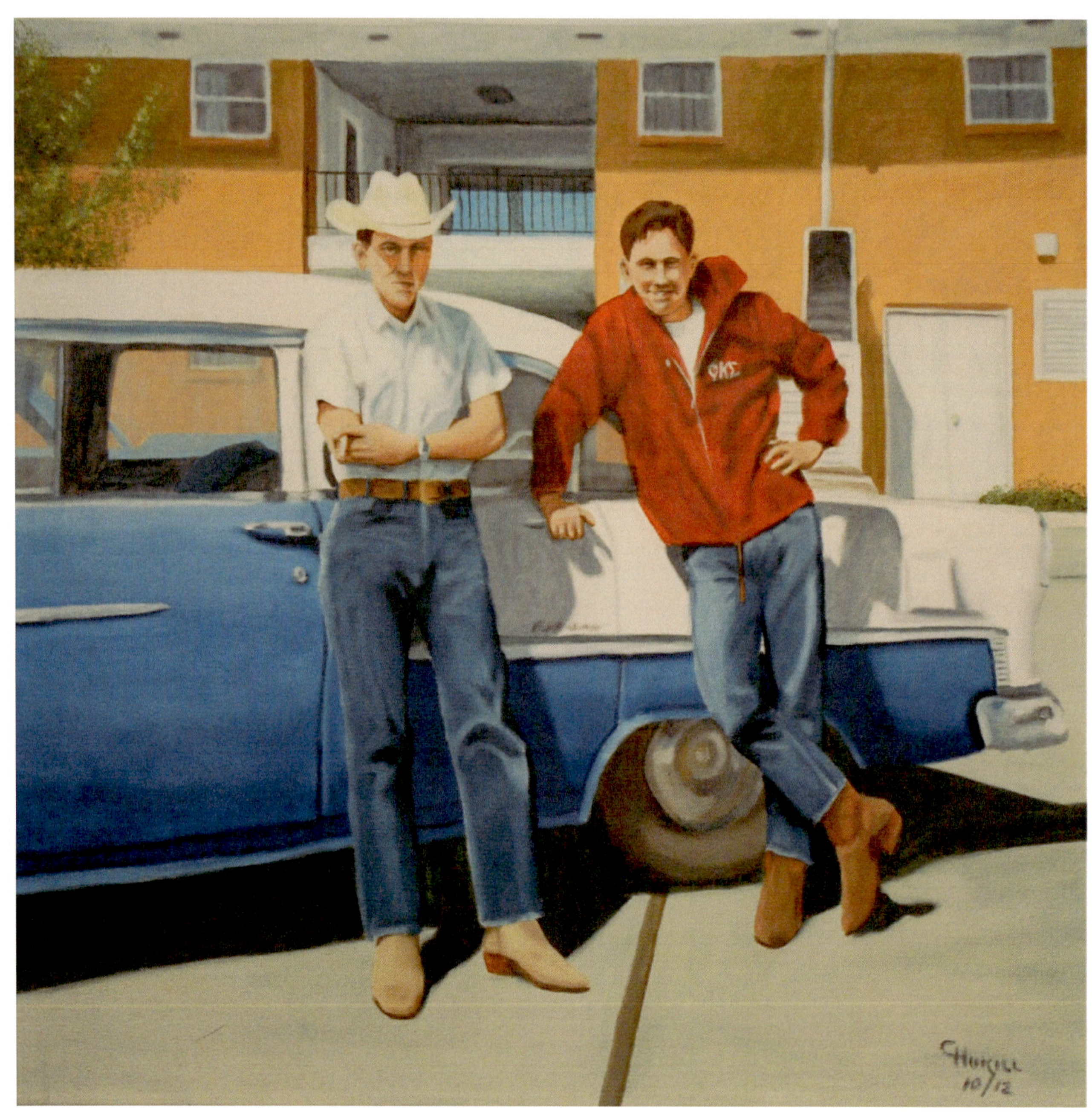

**DOUBLE TROUBLE, 24X24***

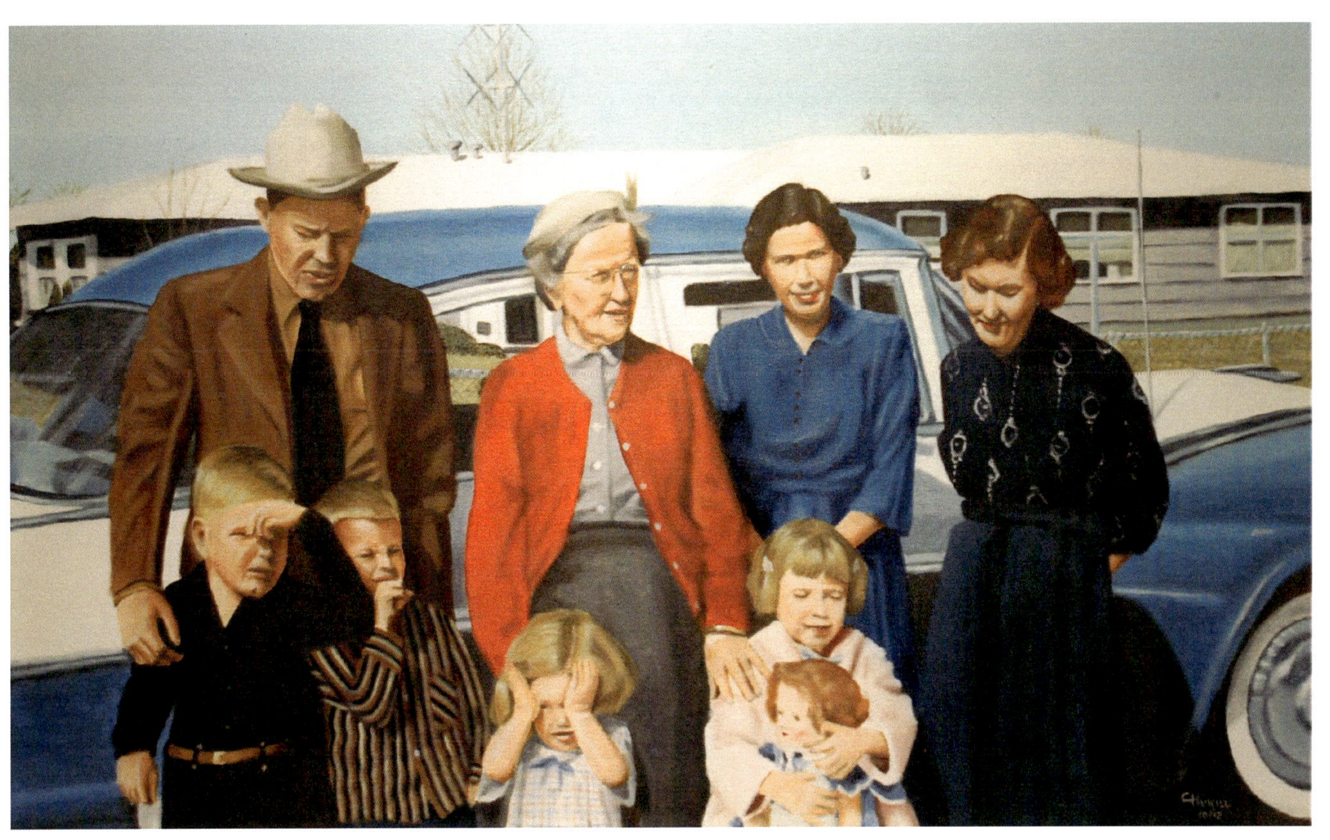

SMILE, 24X36*

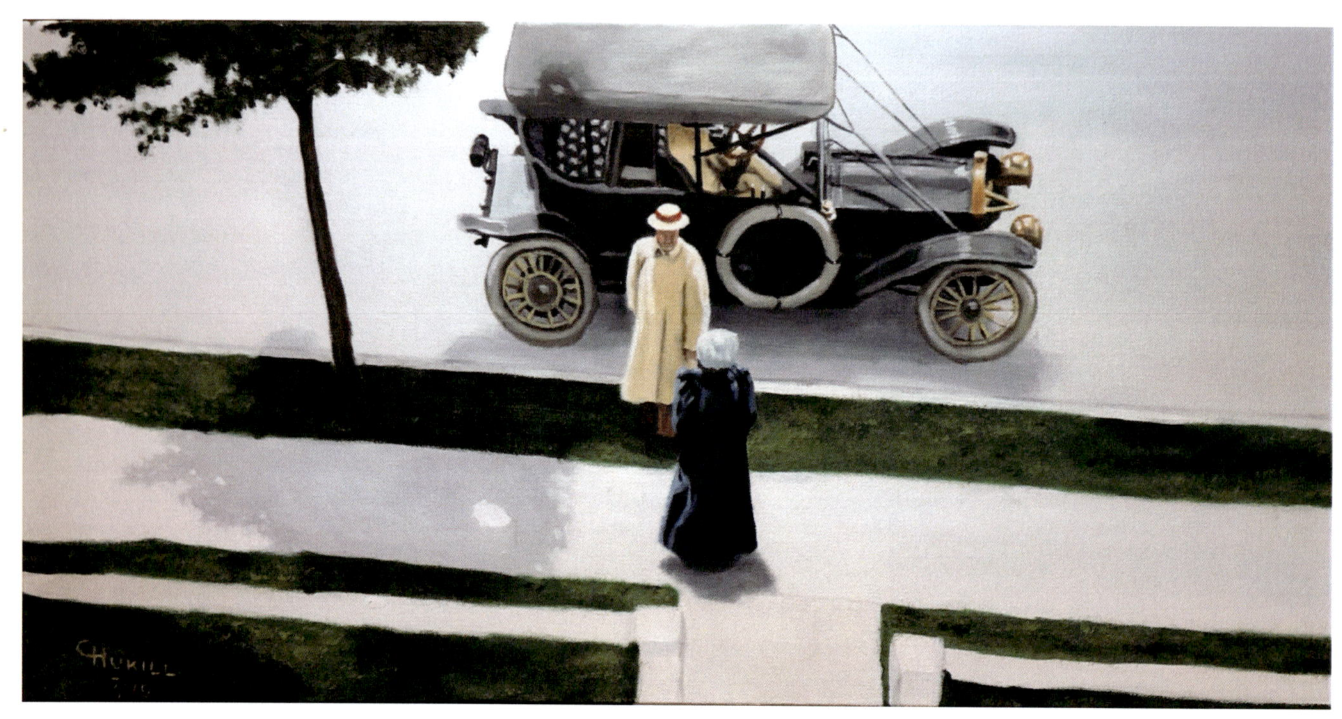

BIRD'S EYE VIEW, 12X24

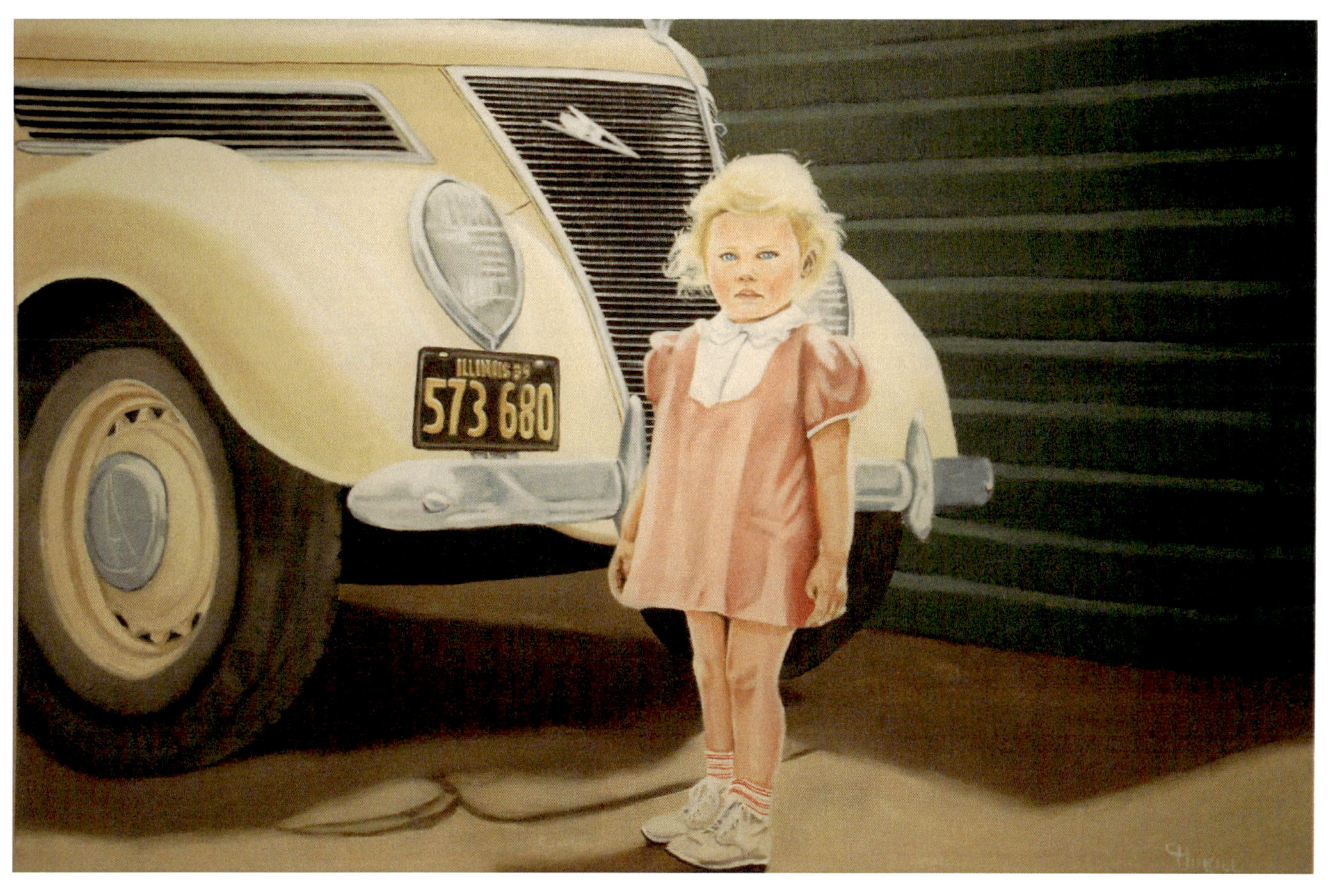


ANGEL WITH AN ATTITUDE, 24X36

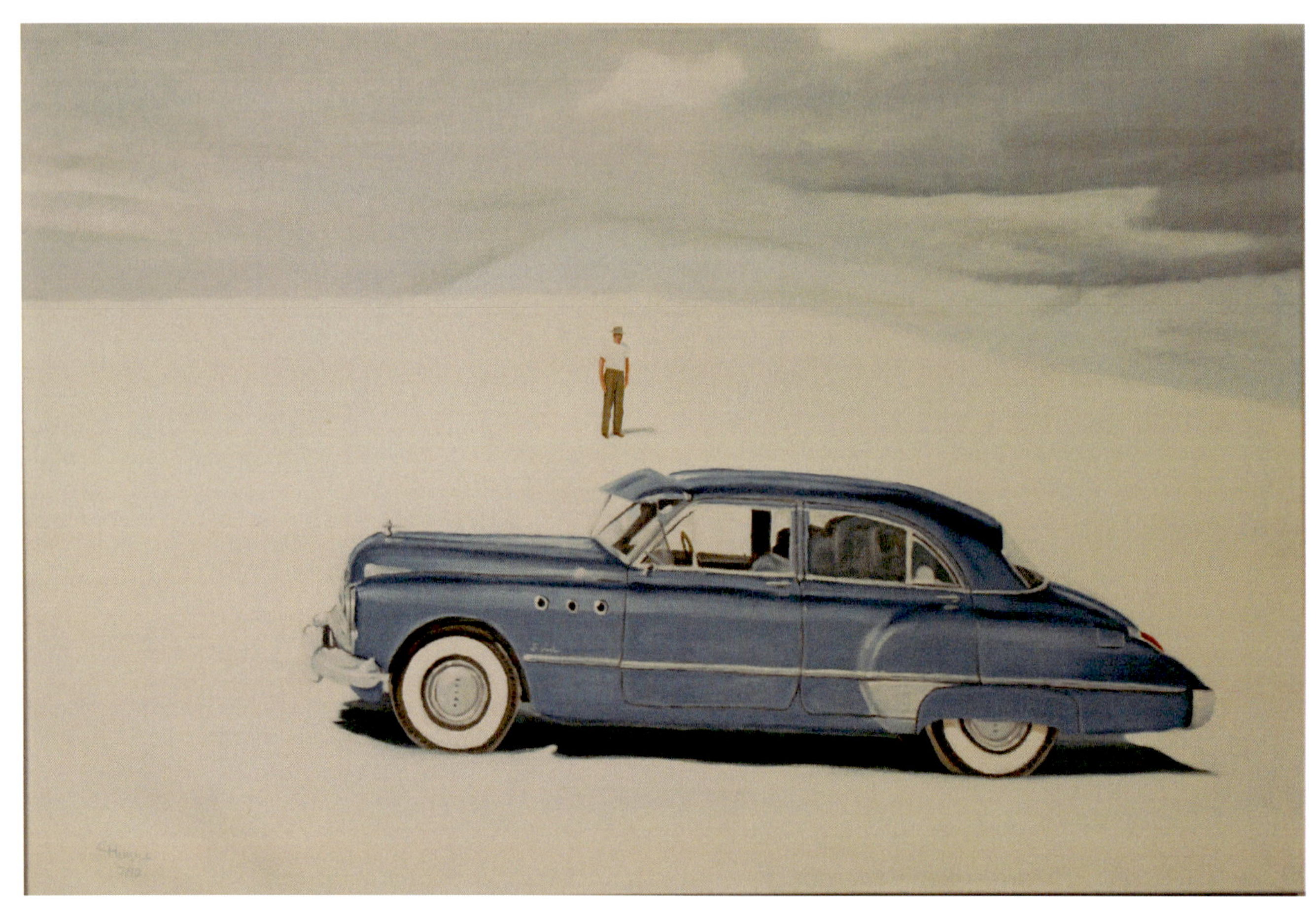

**CAR, MAN, SKY, SAND, 24X36***

# Cell Me a Story

These images were selected specifically for their narrative potential. I believe it's easy to derive a story of some kind from each of them. The titles are intended to encourage the imagination.

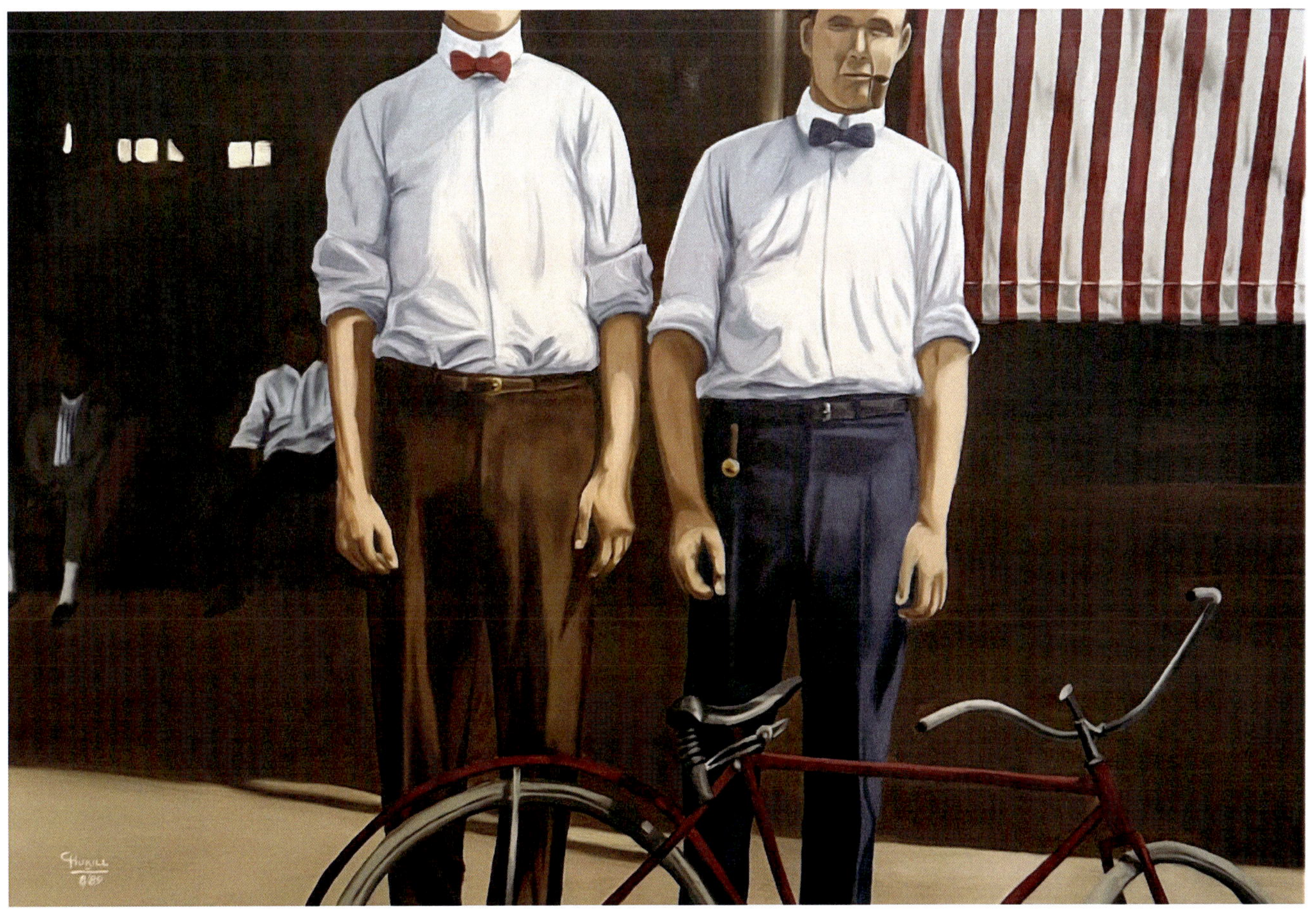

**BICYCLE, 24X36***

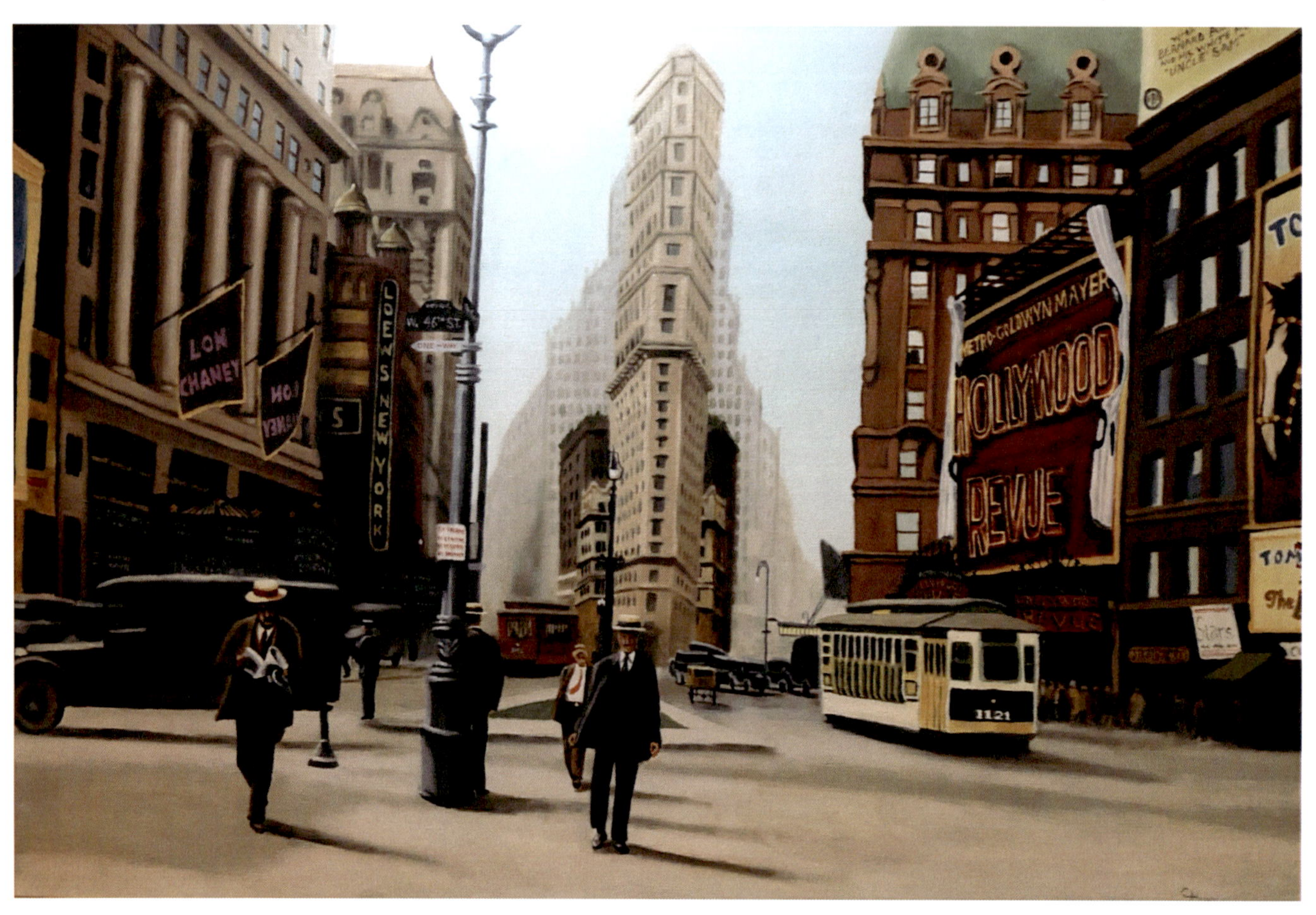


GIVE MY REGARDS TO..., 24X36*

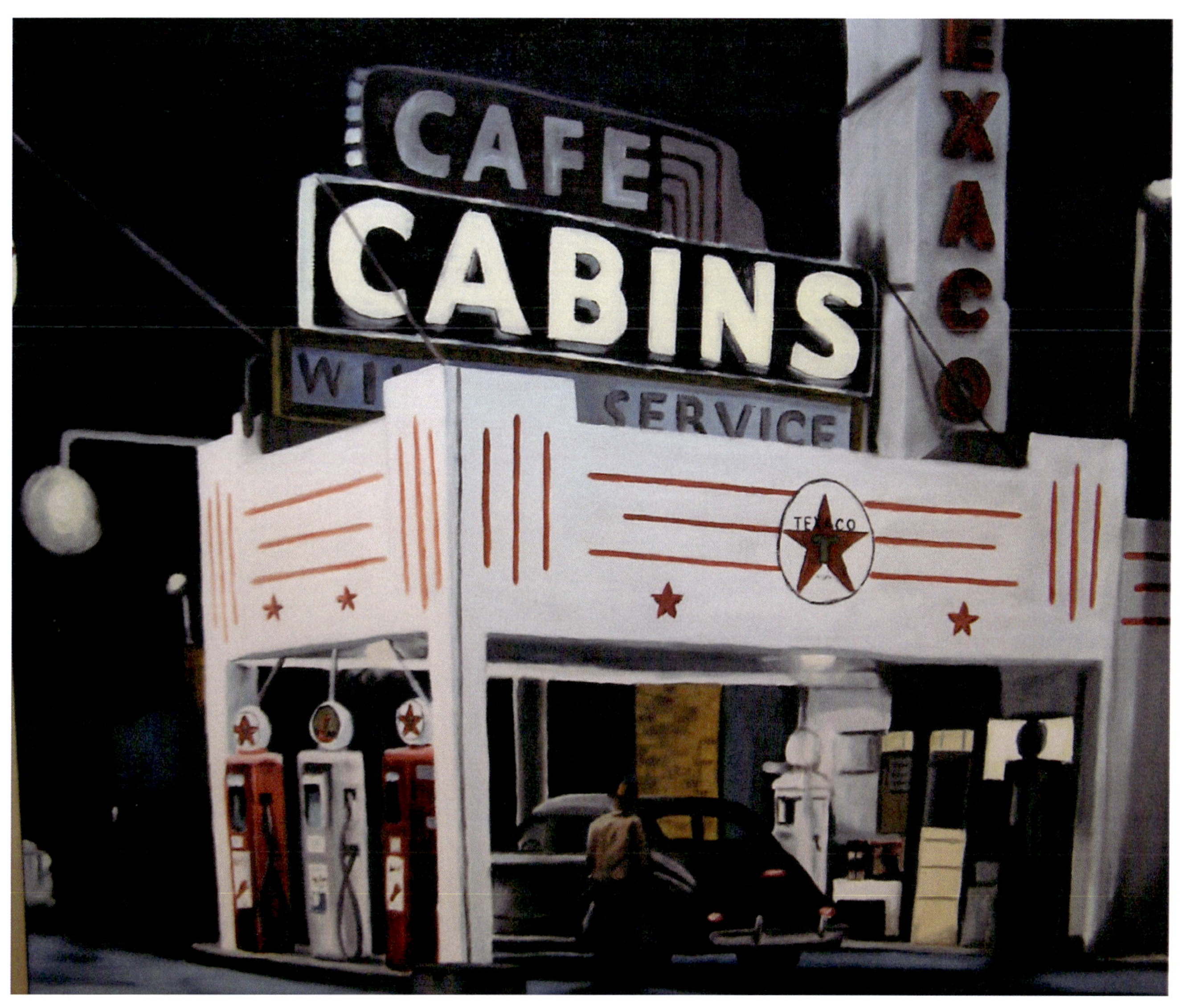


FULL SERVICE, 20X24*

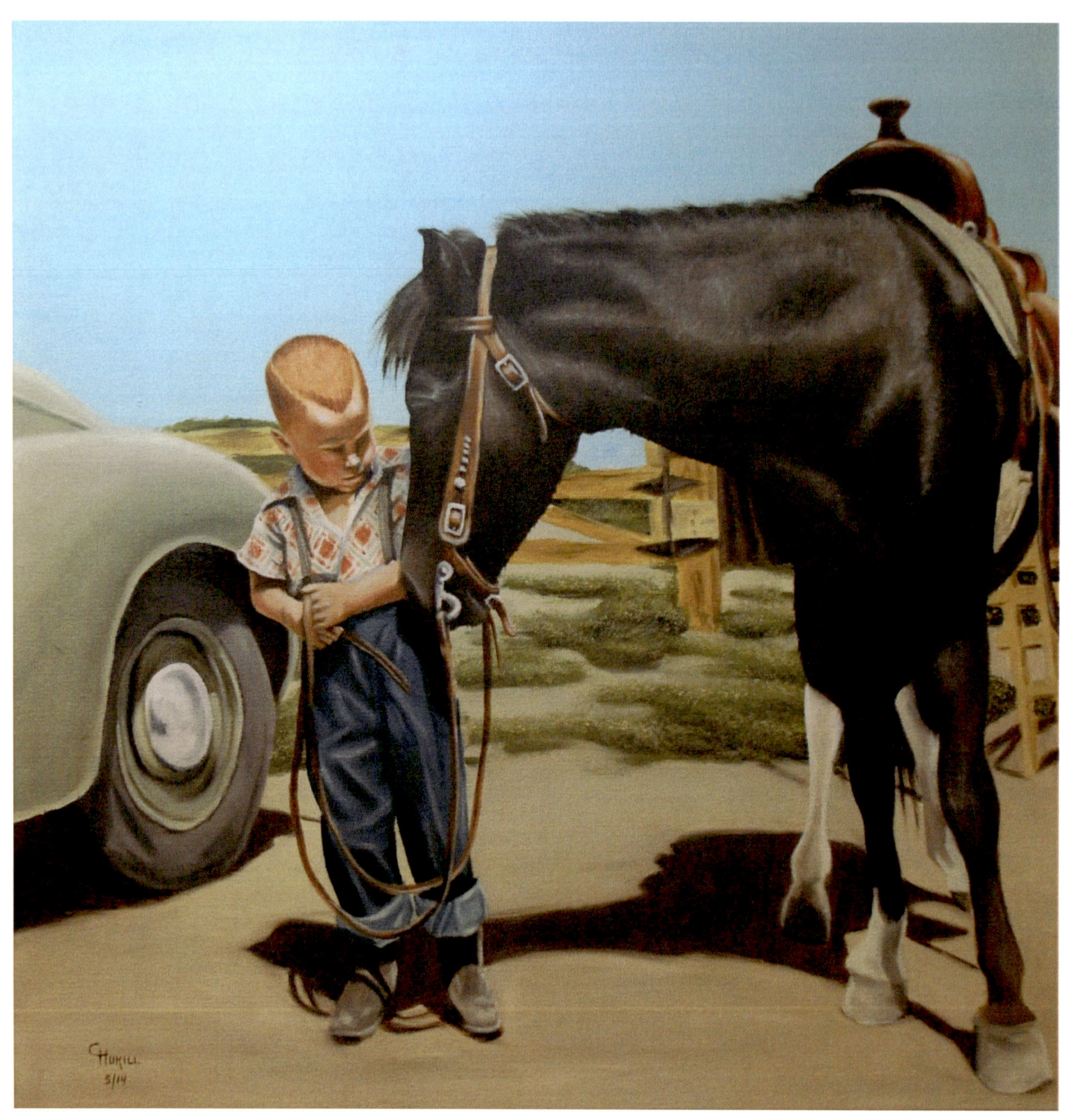

EYE TO EYE, 24X24*

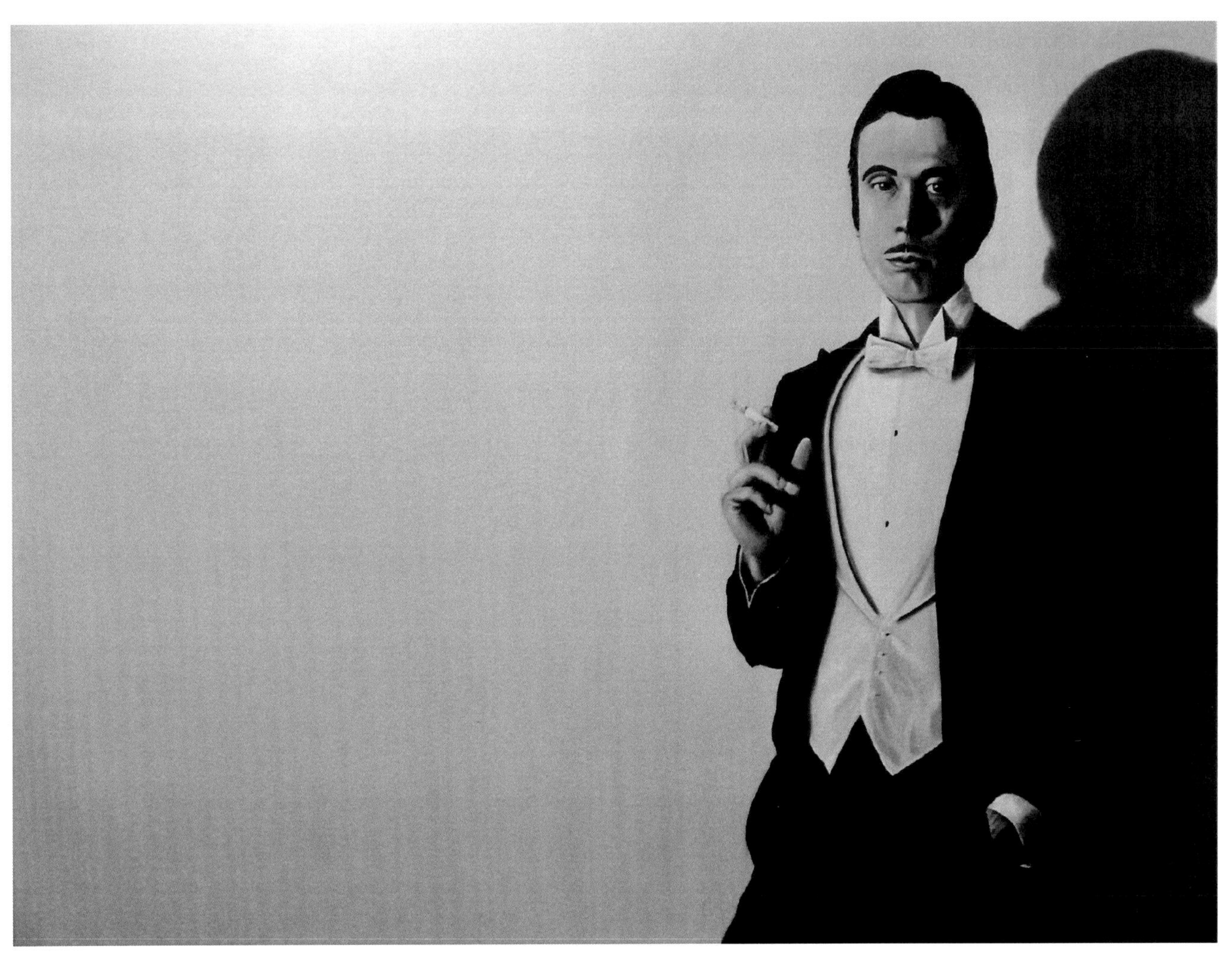

ROCKY DON'T ROCK NO MORE, 30X40*

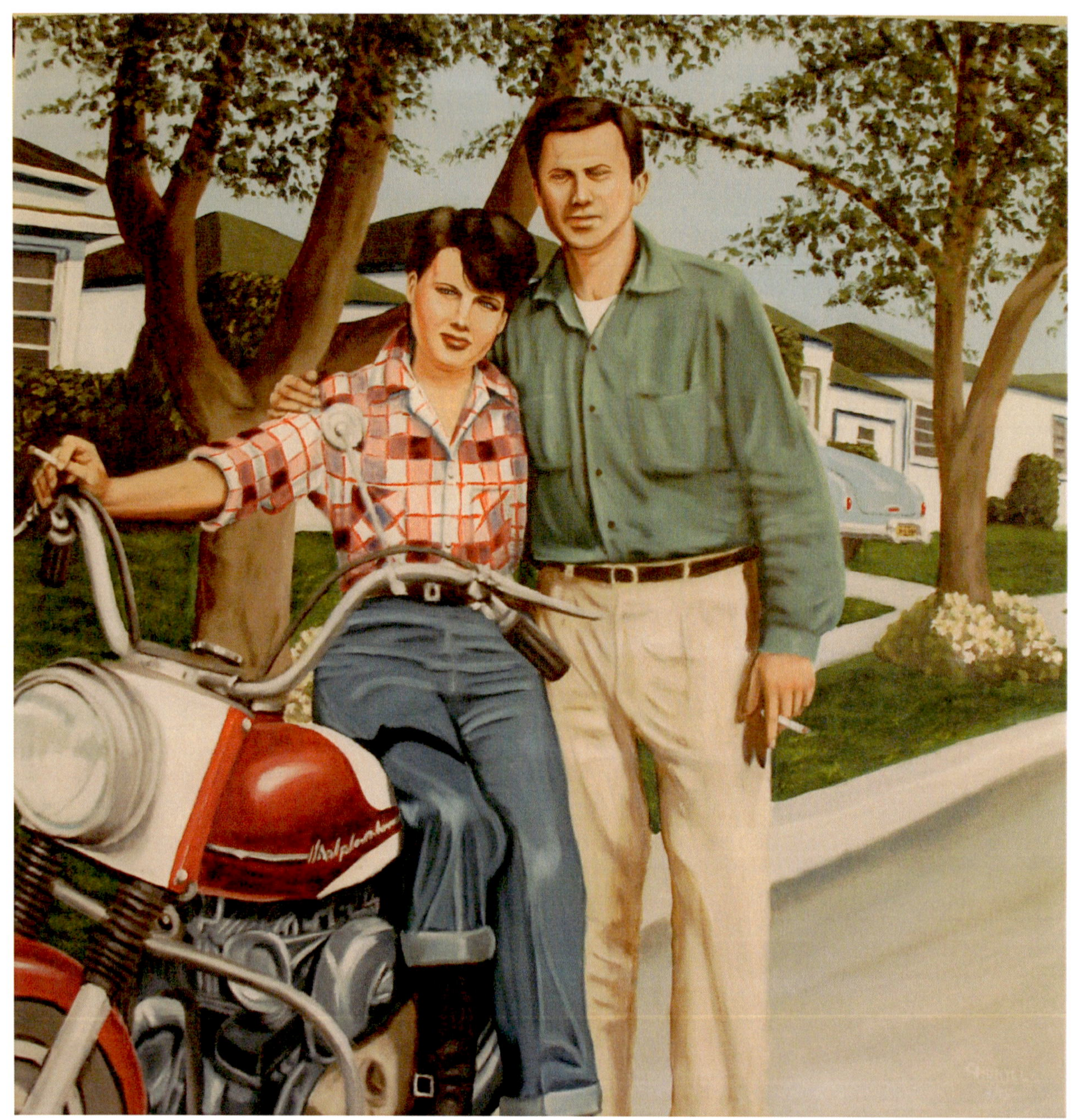

COOL CATS, 30X30

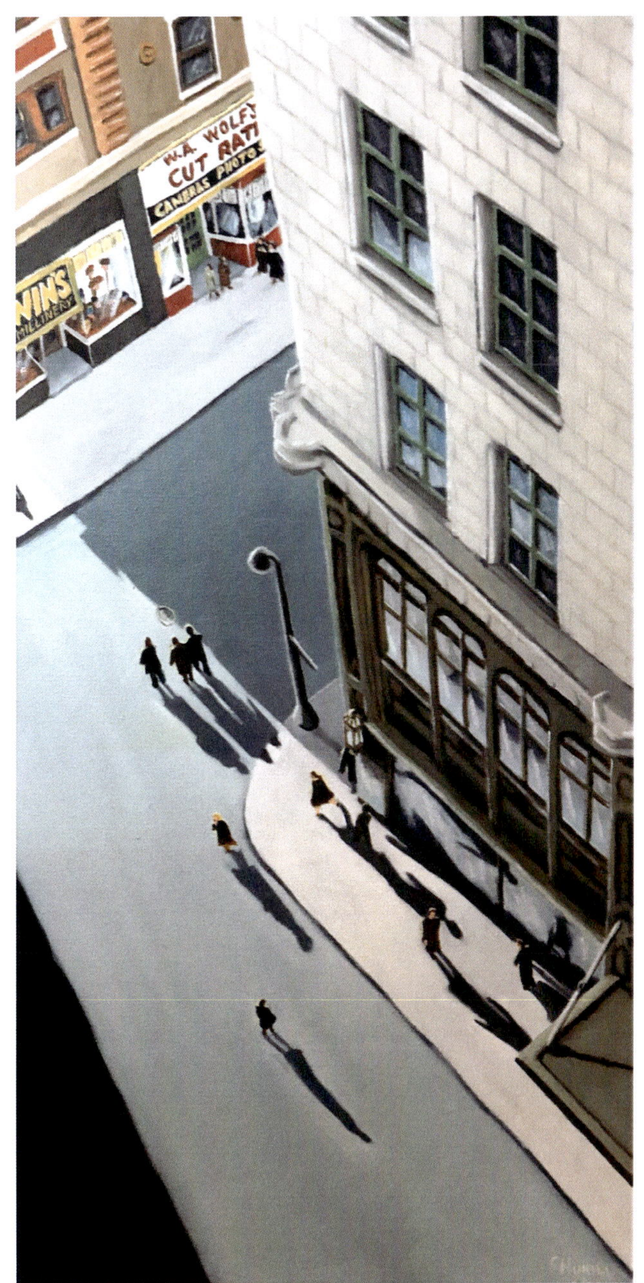


URBAN CANYONLANDS, 15X30

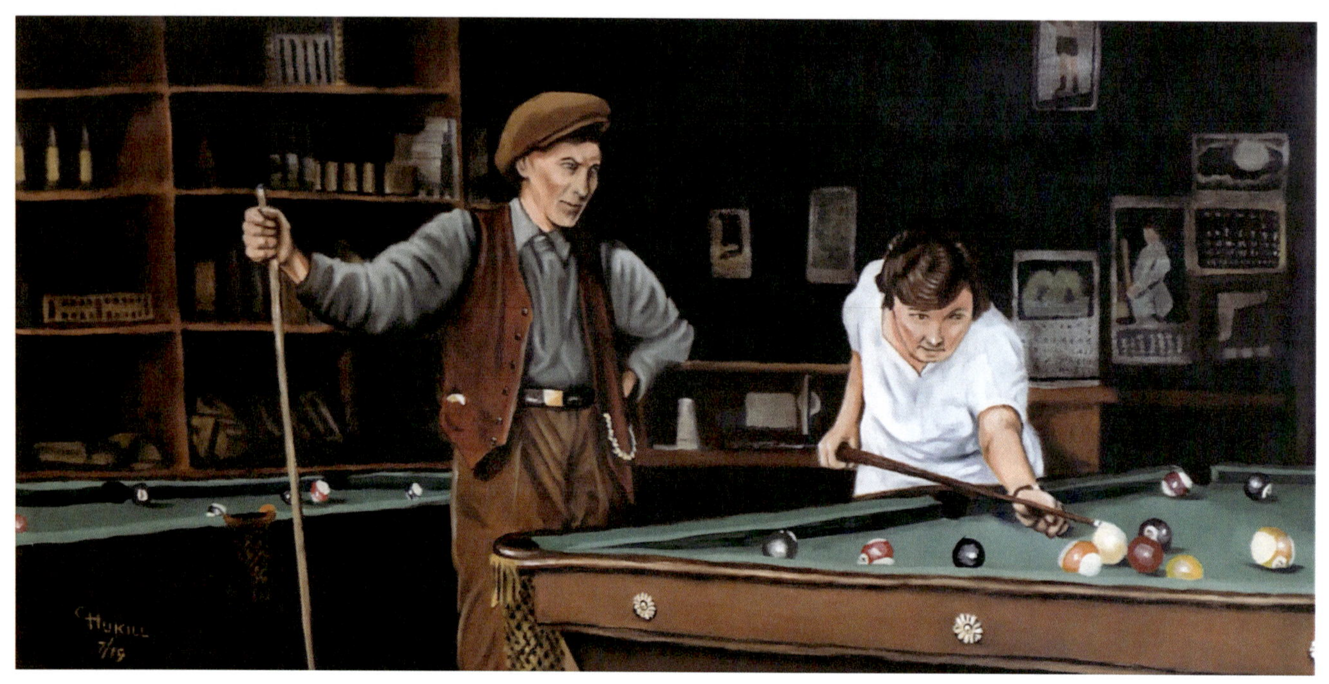

THE HUSTLER, 15X30

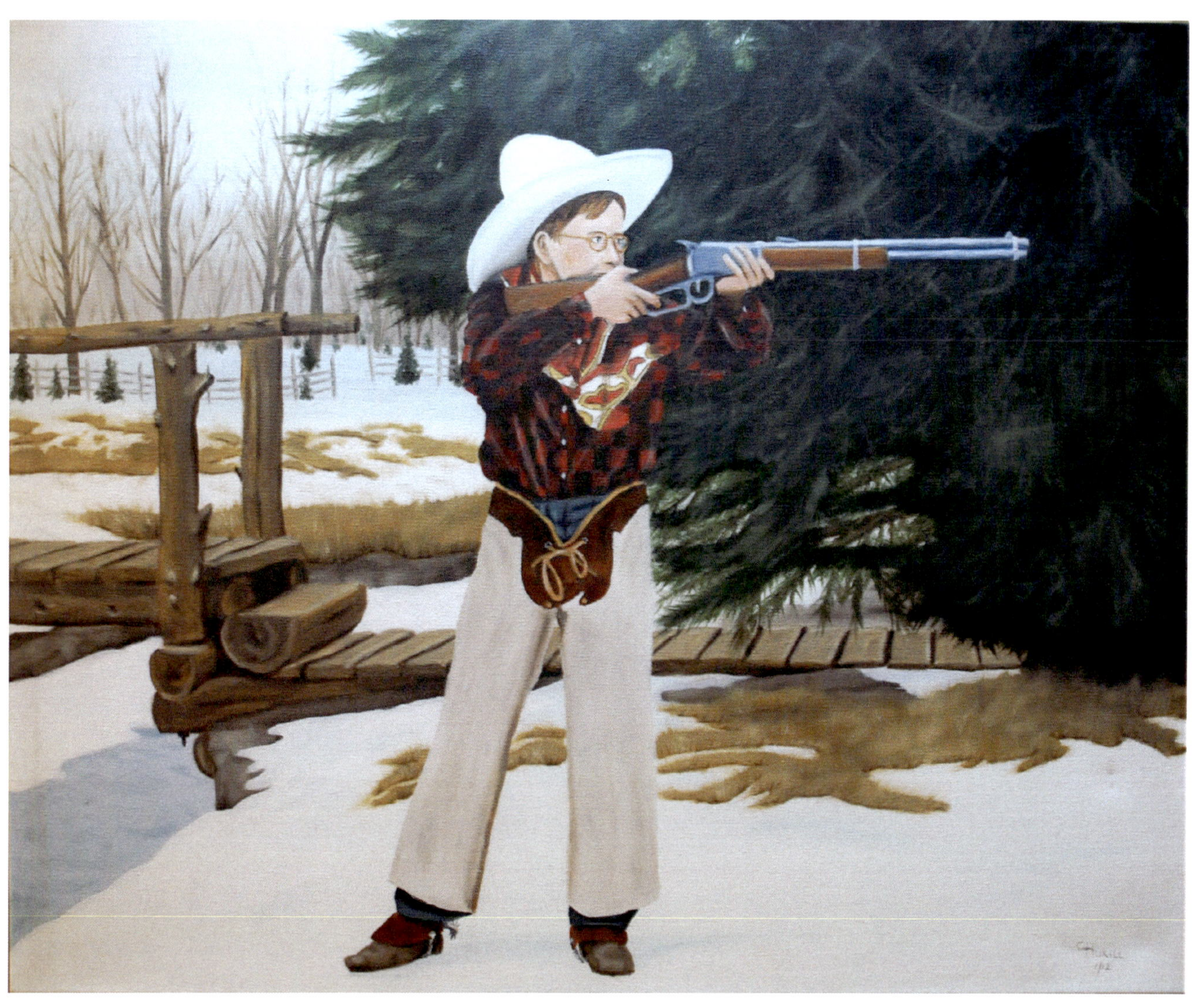

"YOU'LL SHOOT YOUR EYE OUT," 24X30*

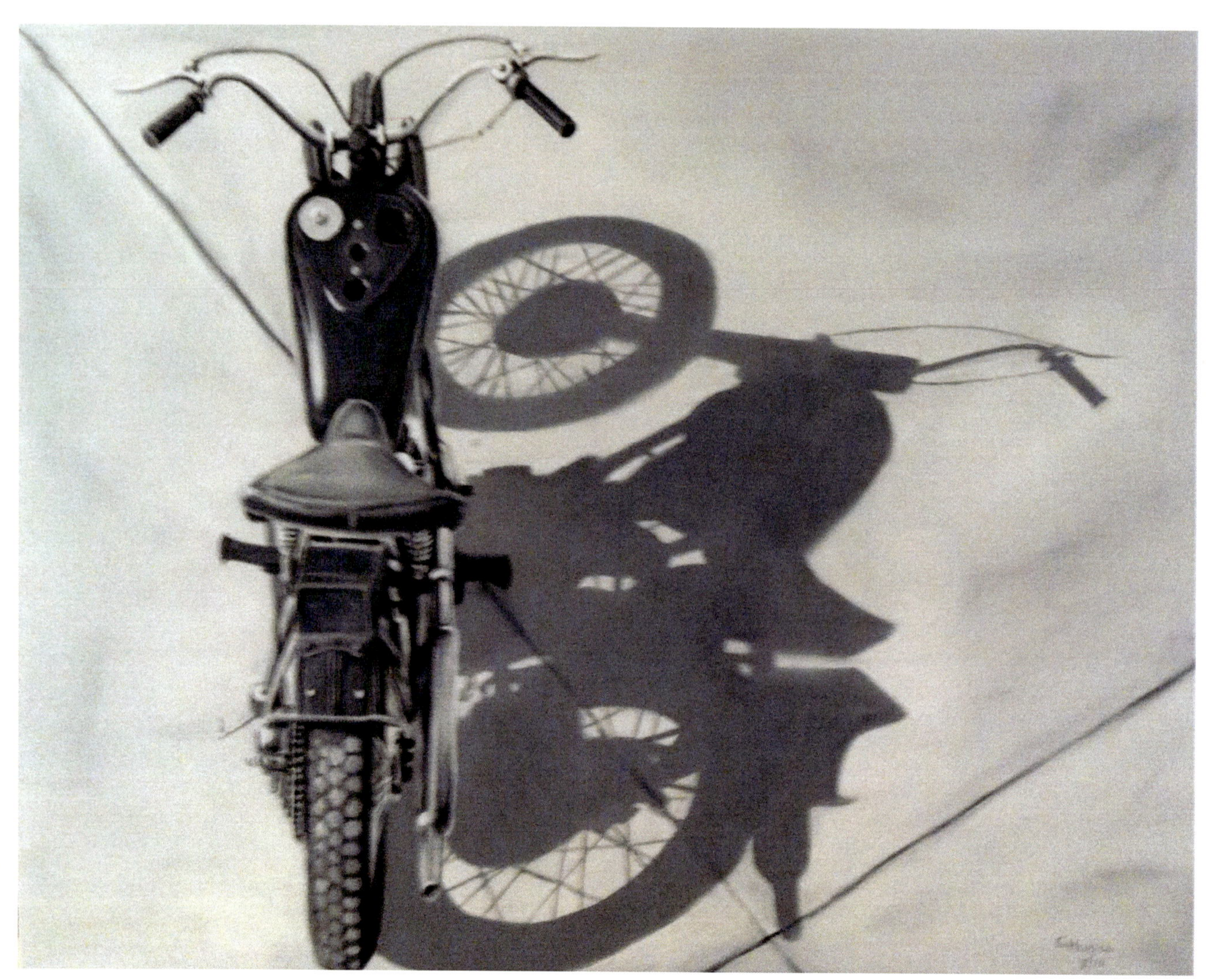

**THE SHADOW, 24X30***

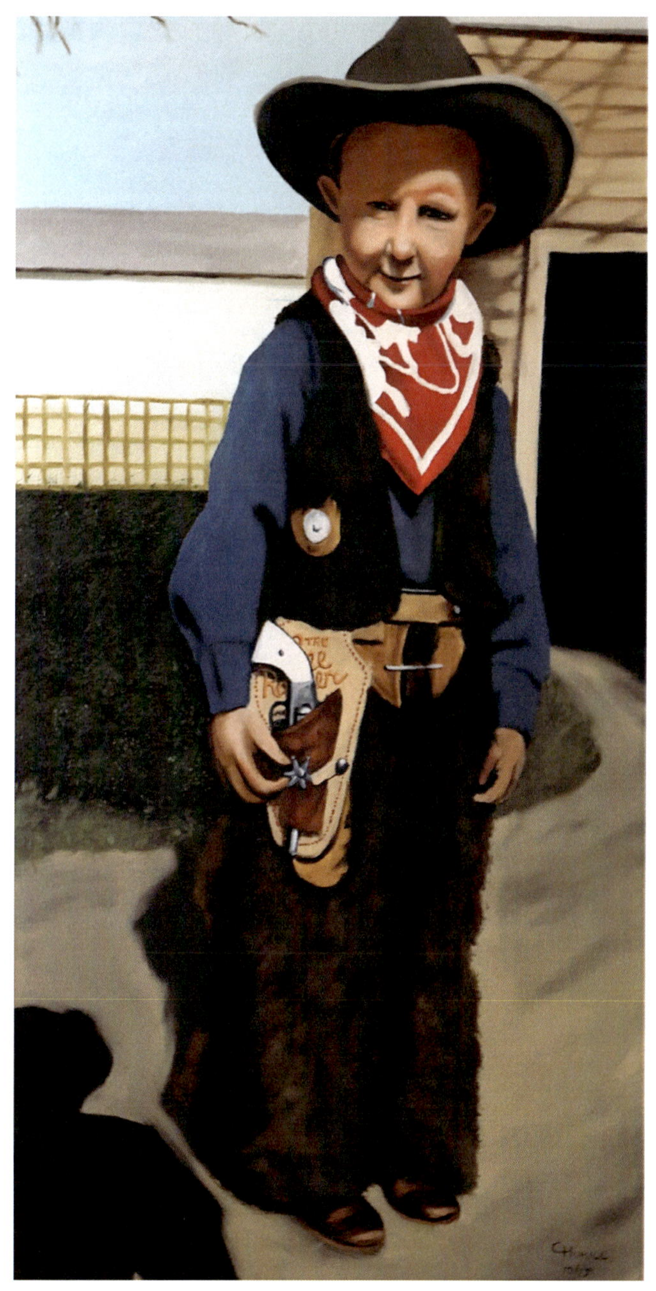

**OPEN CARRY, 1954, 15X30**

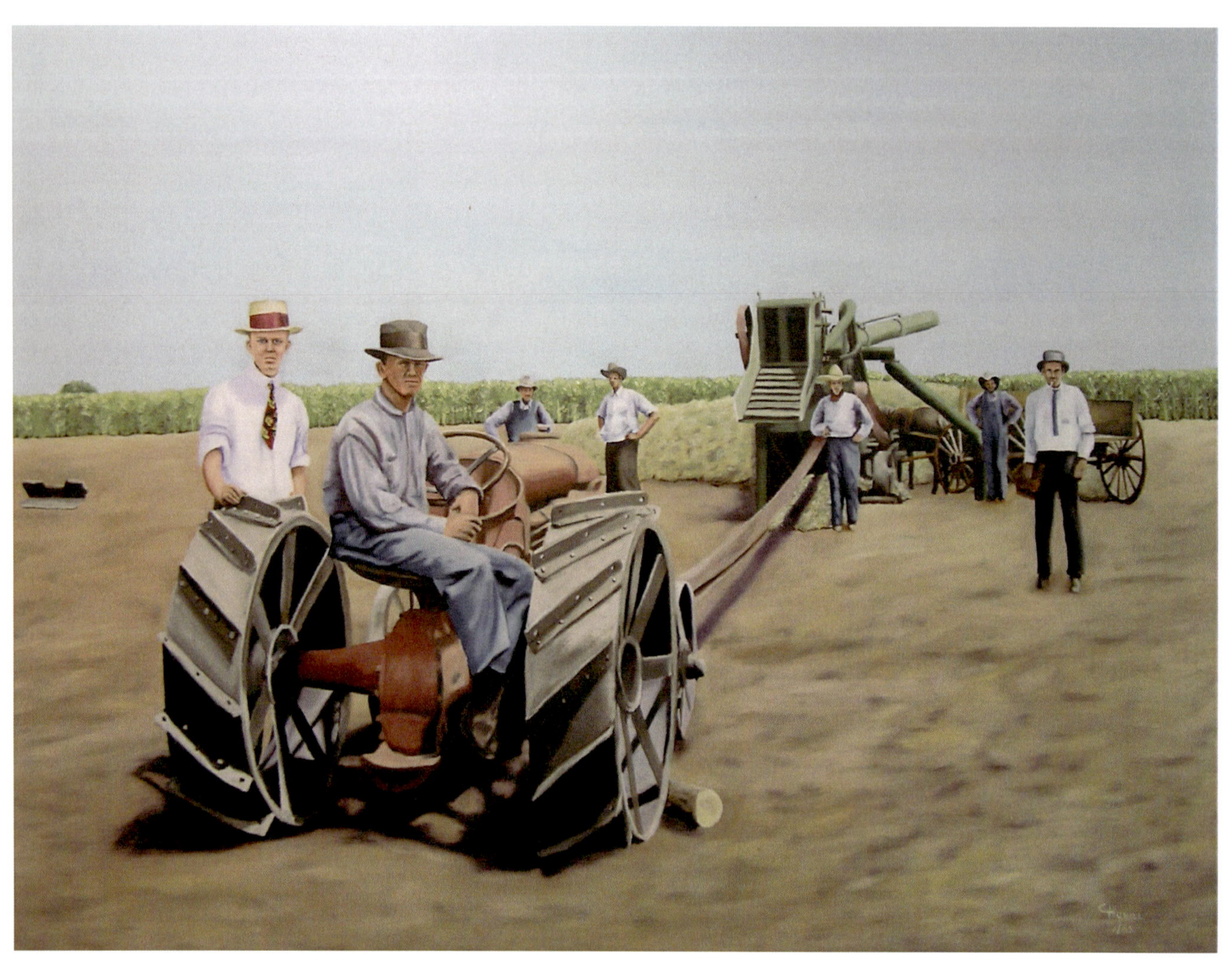

MEN OUT STANDING IN THEIR FIELD, 30X40

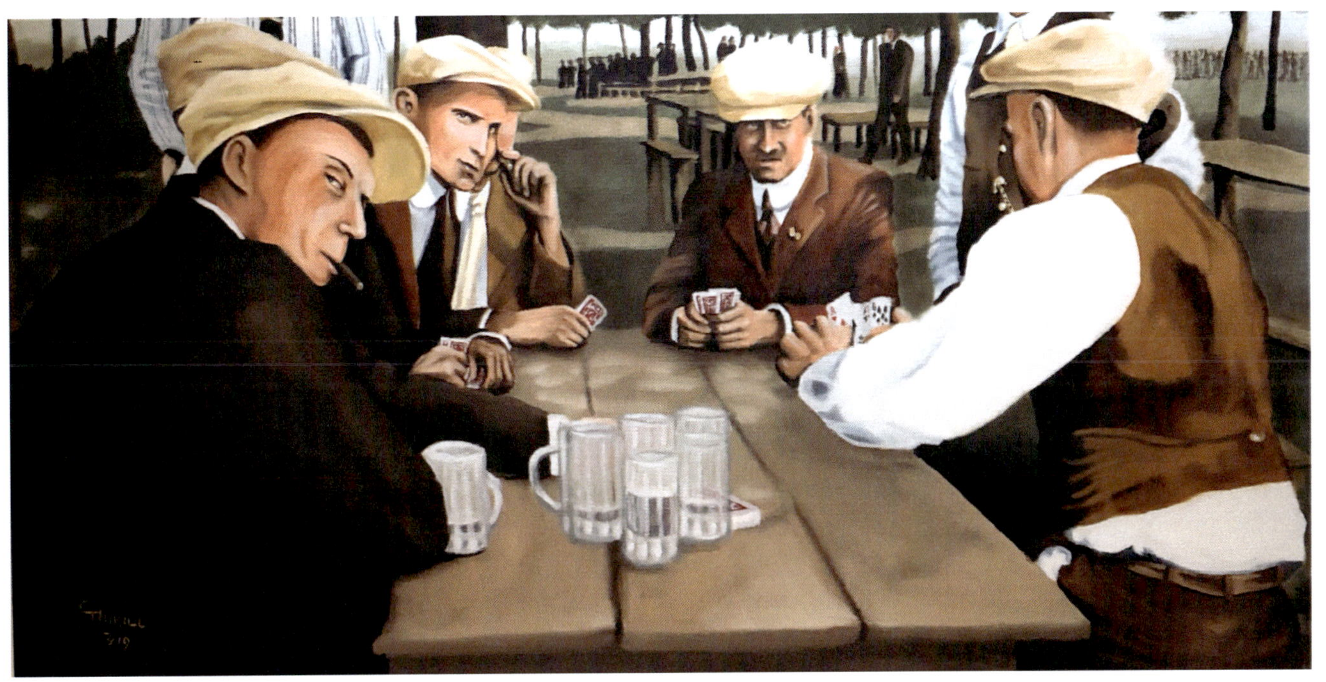

THE CARD PLAYERS, 15X30

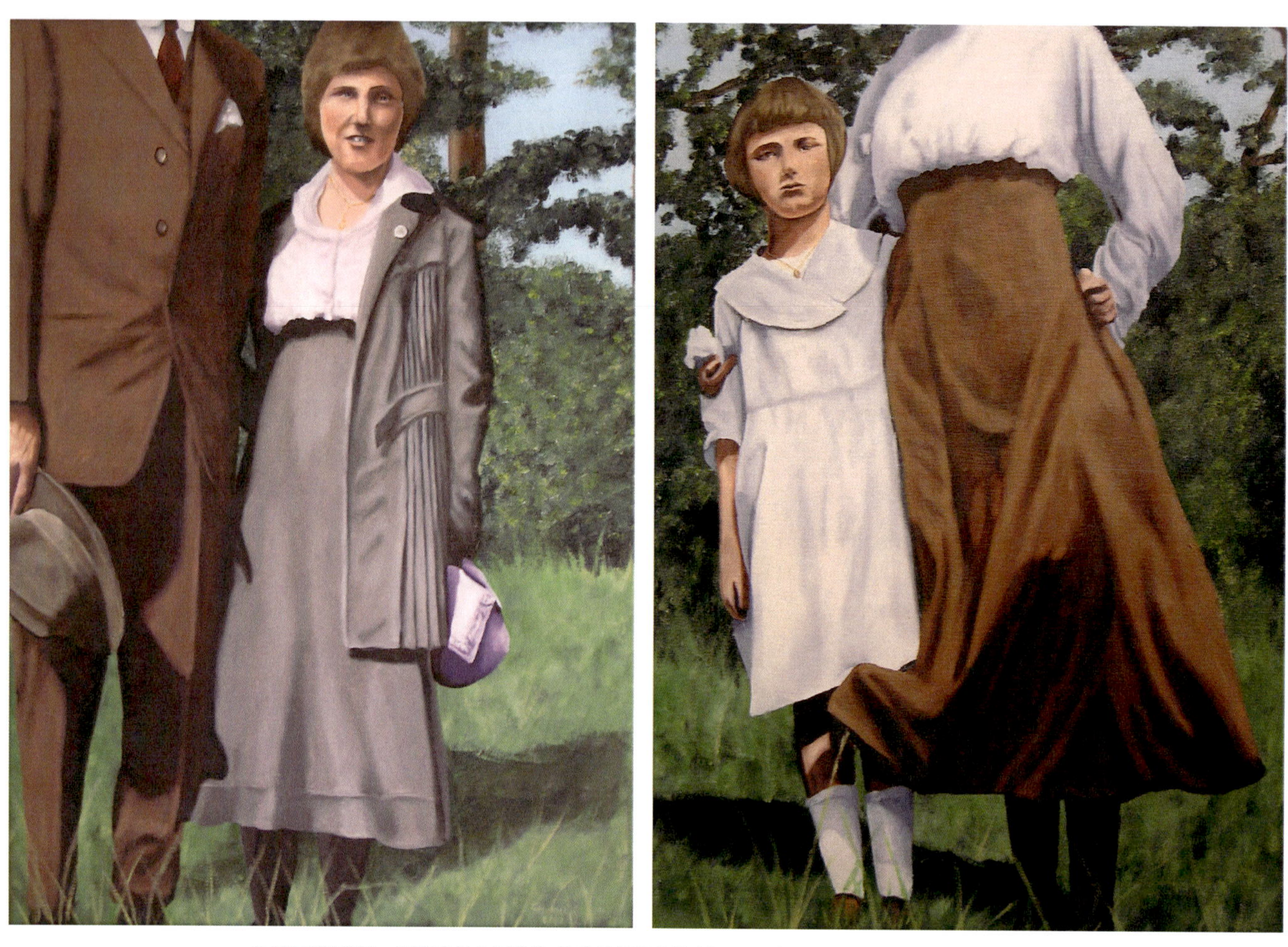

DIPTYCH: HEADLESS PORTRAITS #1 & #2, 18X24 EACH*

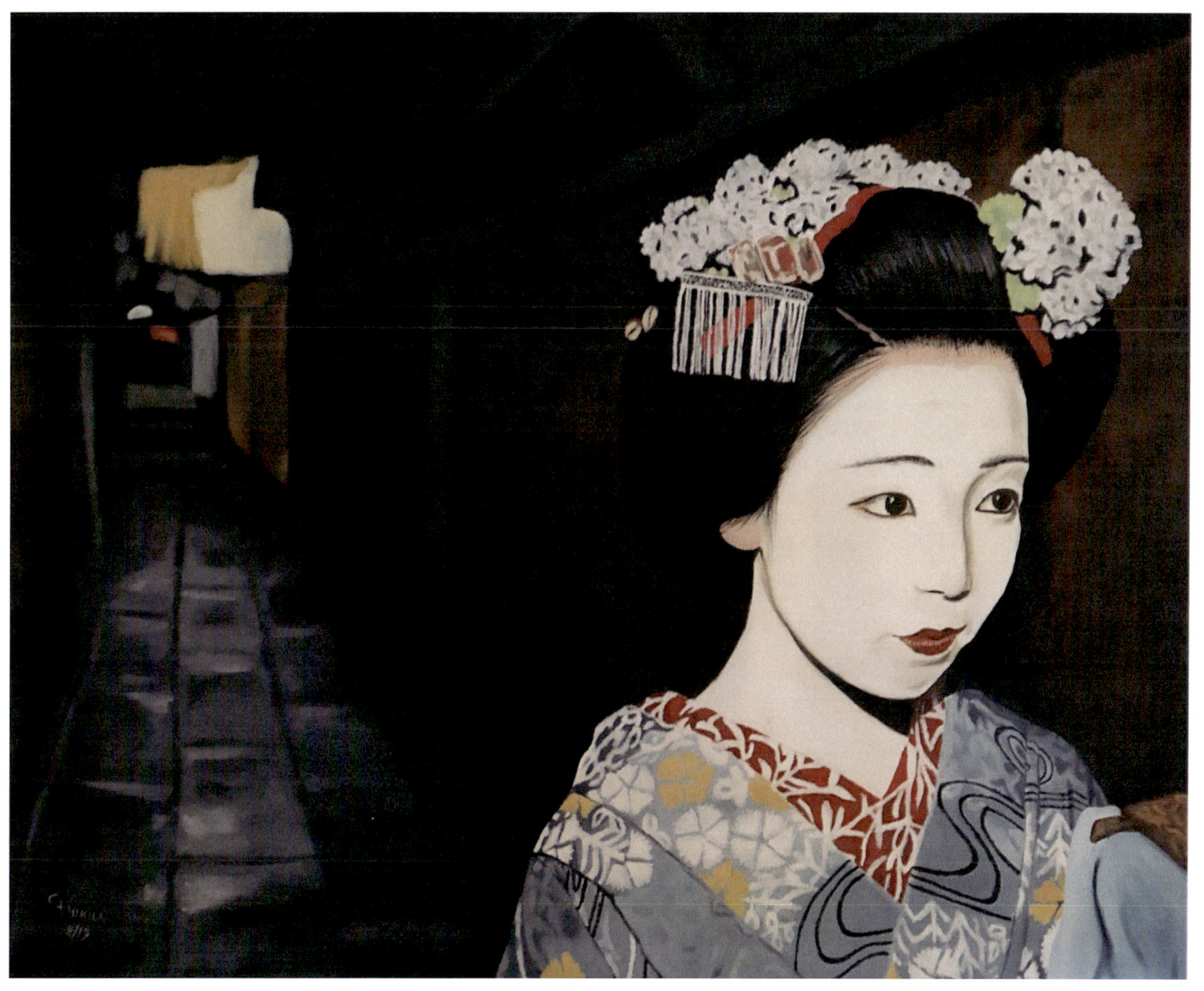

BACKSTAGE GEISHA, 24X30

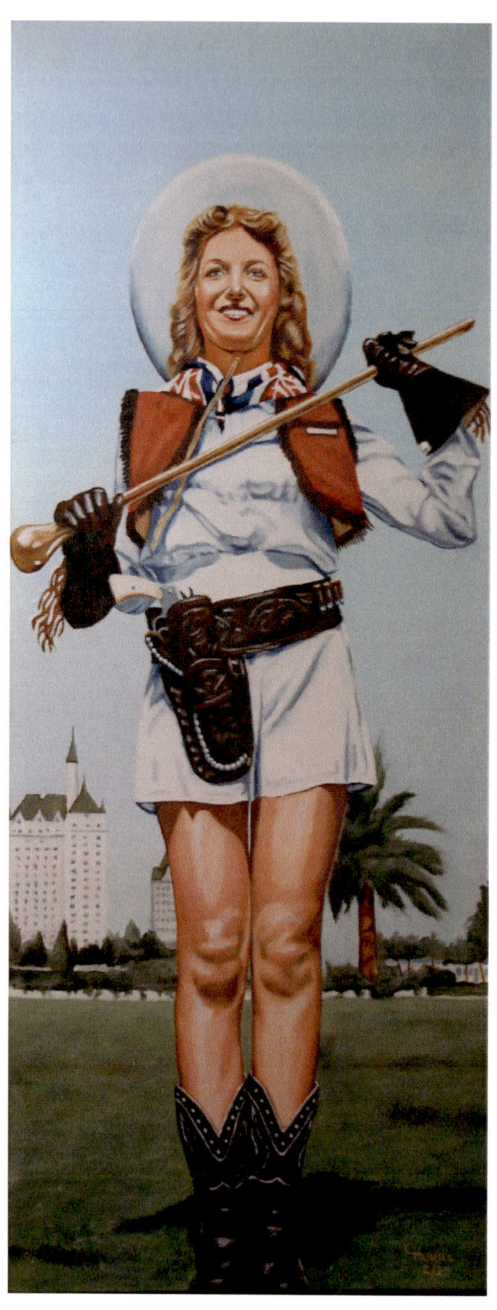

ARMED, LEGGED, AND DANGEROUS, 20X40

# Four-Legged Family Members

In 2016 I had a show entitled "The Best Deal" at the Center for Contemporary Arts concentrating on images of people and their dogs. Another example of Americana in my work. It has been said that the domestication of dogs was the best deal humans ever made. Humans give dogs their leftover time, leftover food, and leftover love. In return, dogs give humans everything.

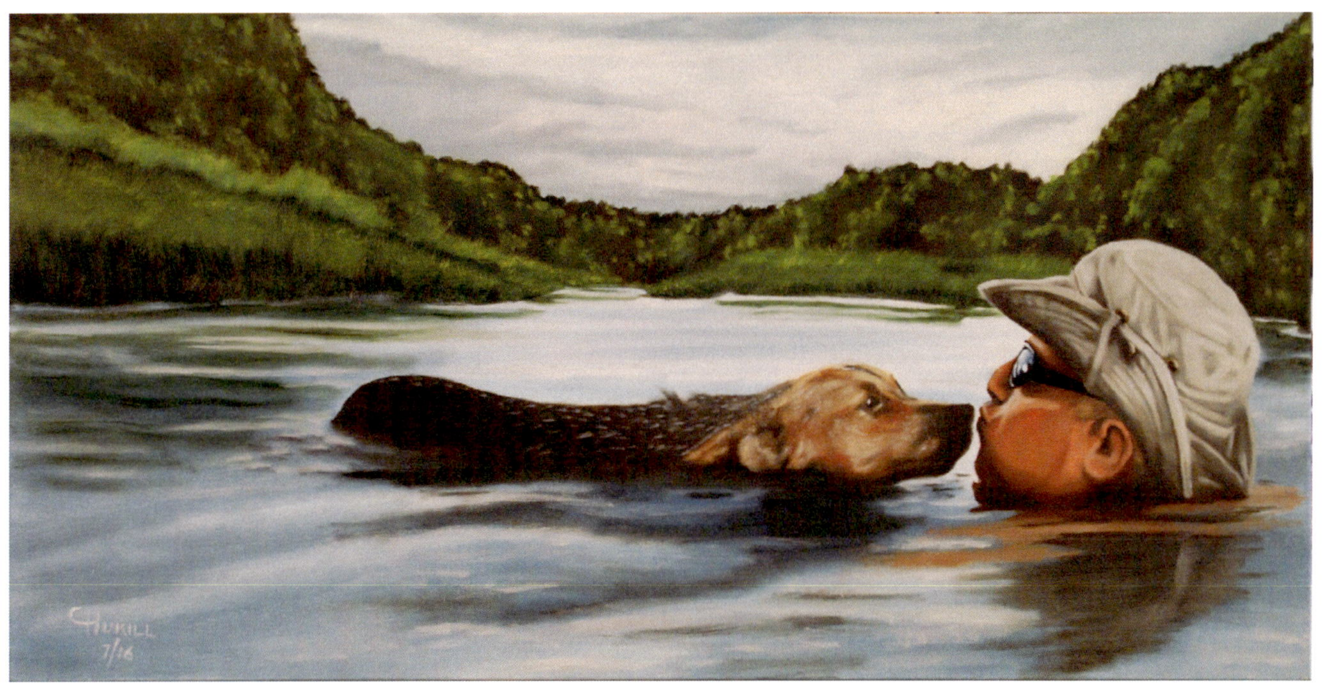

**"GIVE US A KISS," 15X30***

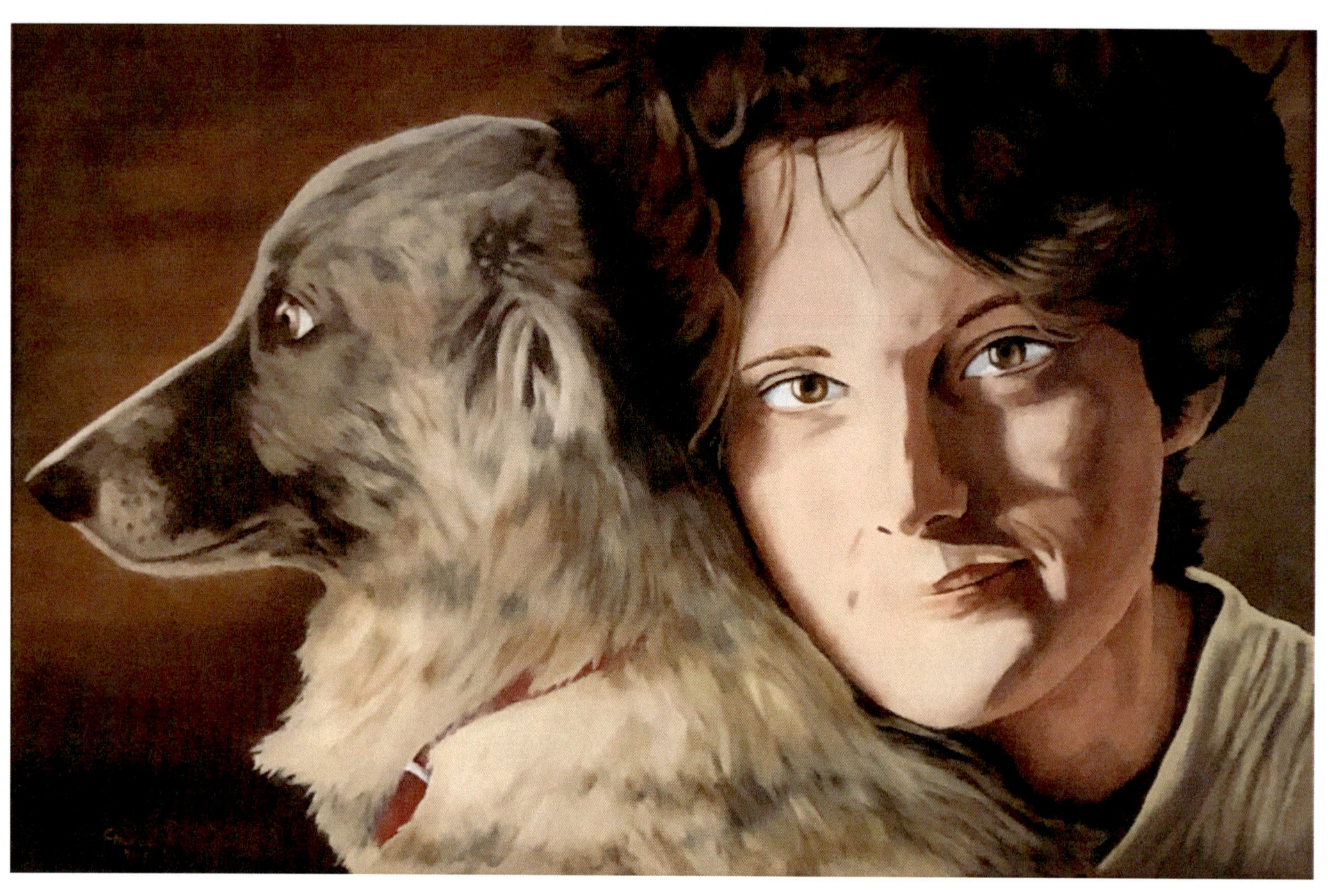

BET #2: WITH ROCKY, 24X36*

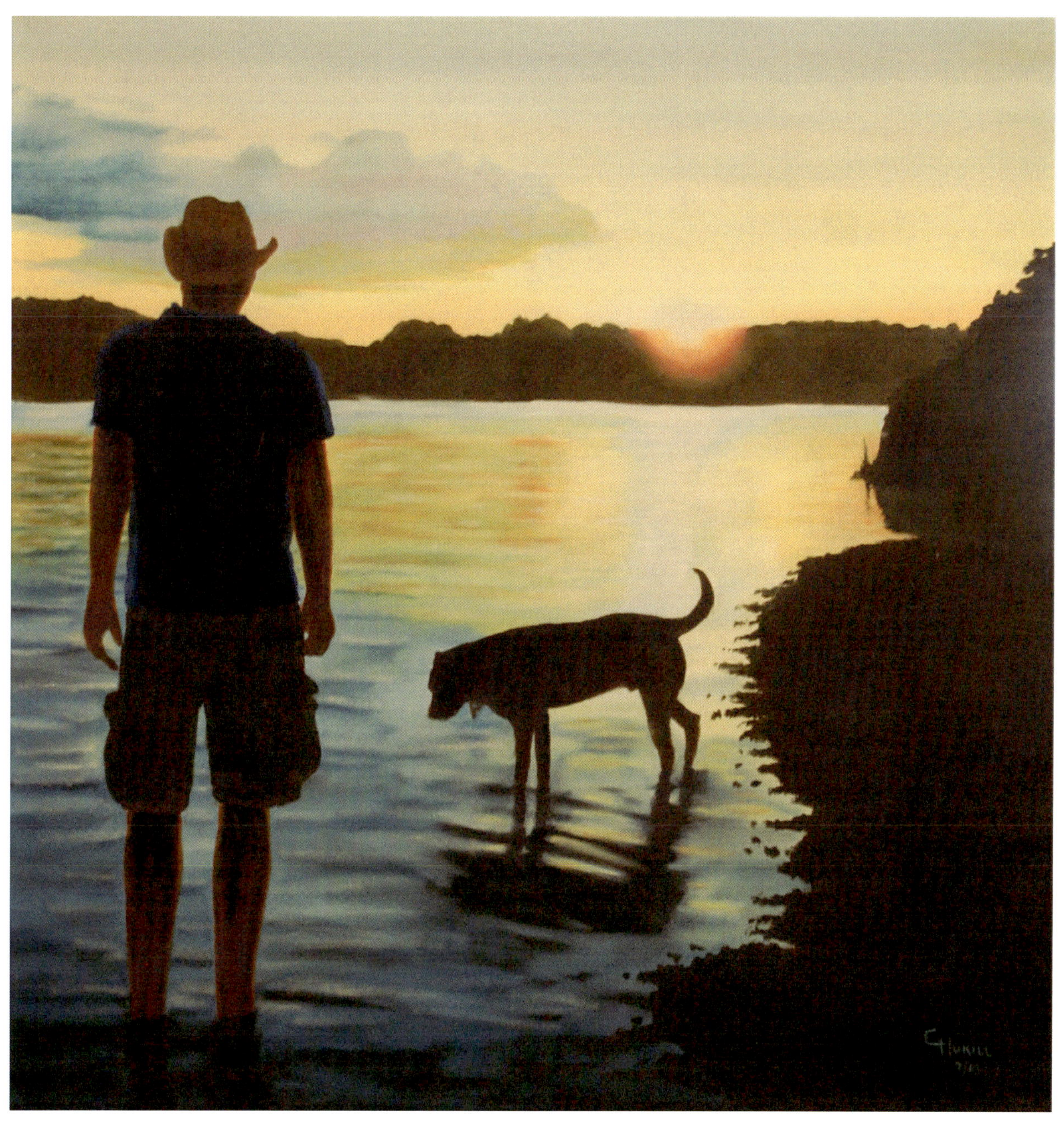

BARRY AND LEFTY, 24X24*

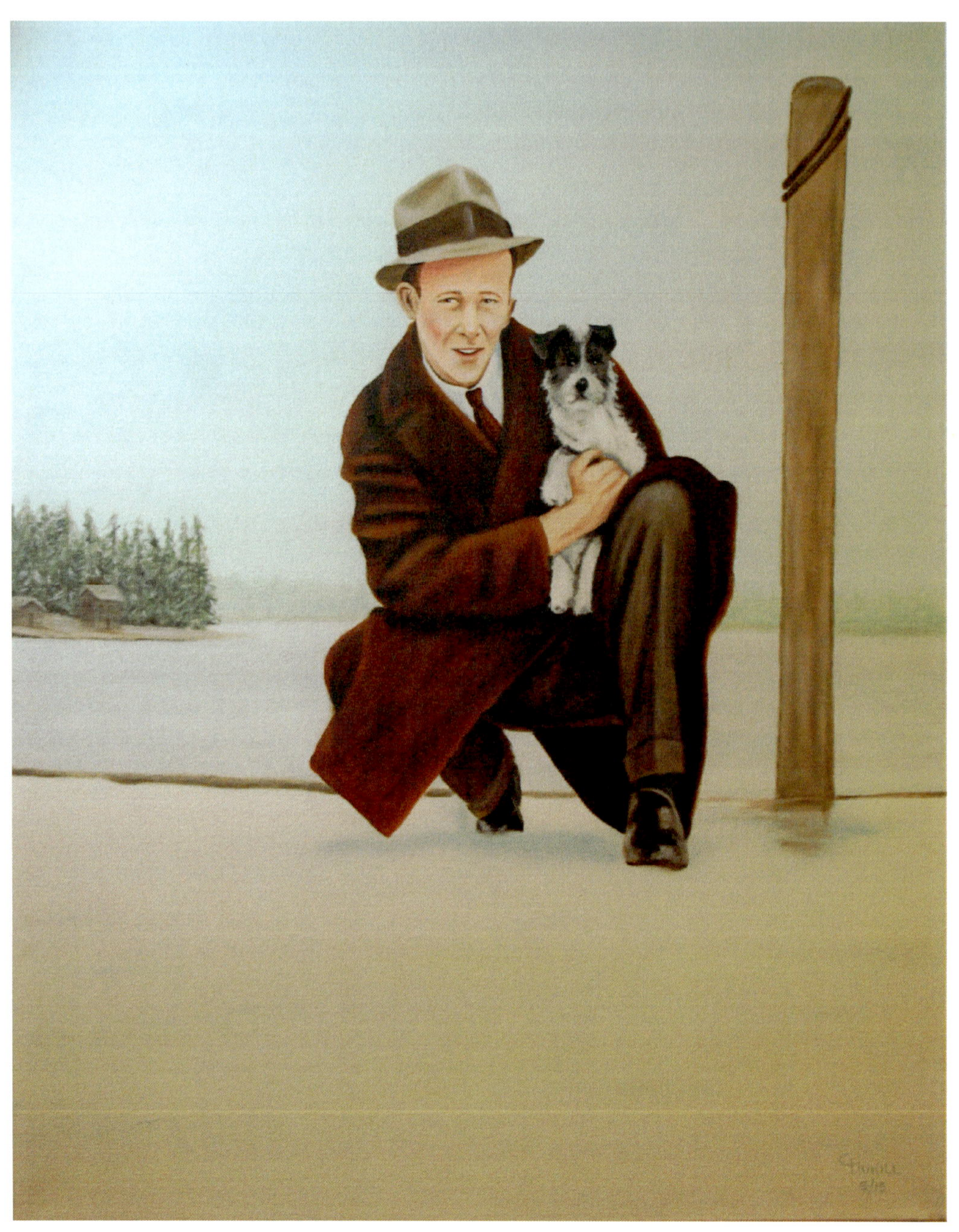

**COMFORT IN THE COLD, 24X30**

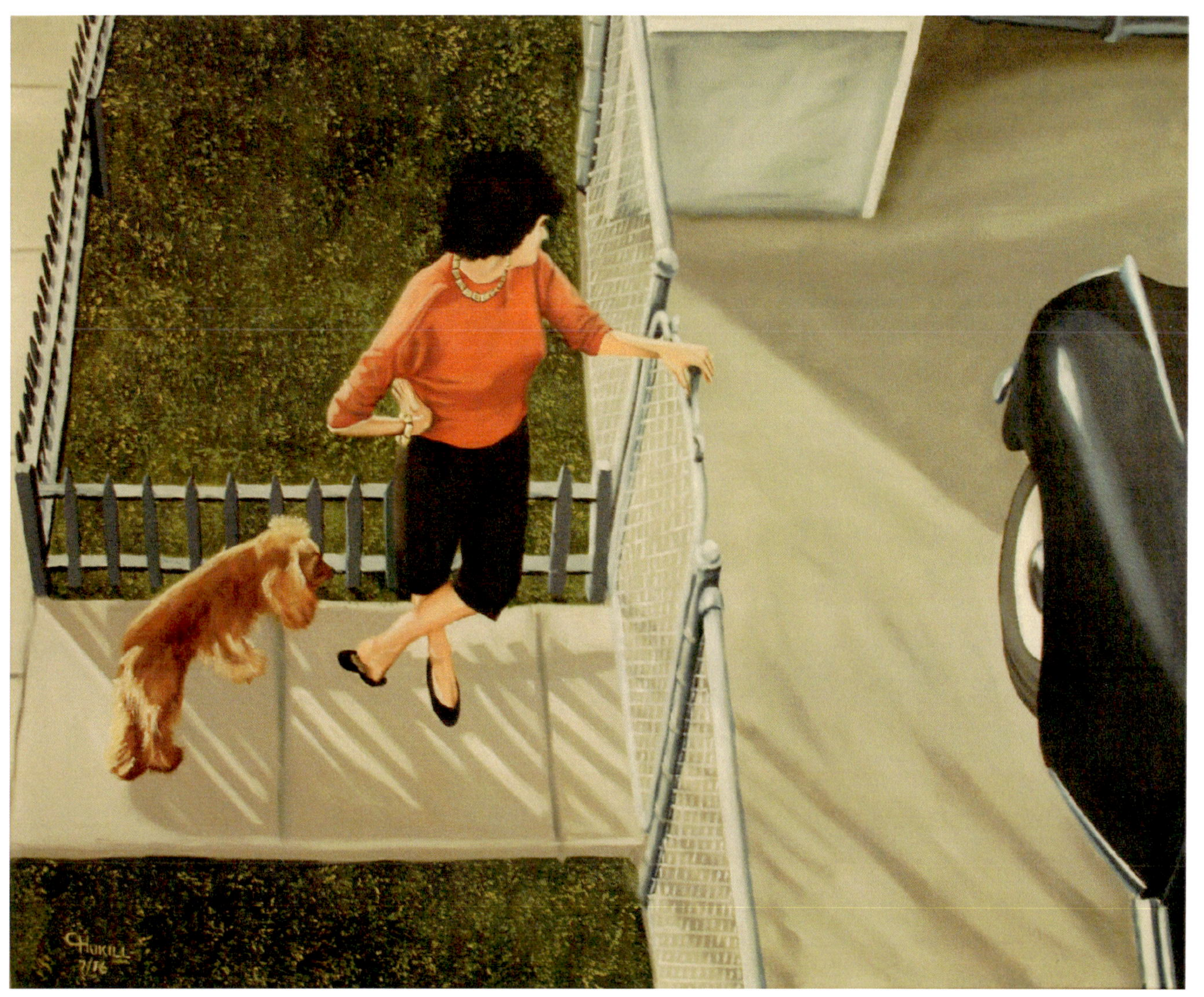

A CAT'S EYE VIEW, 18X24*

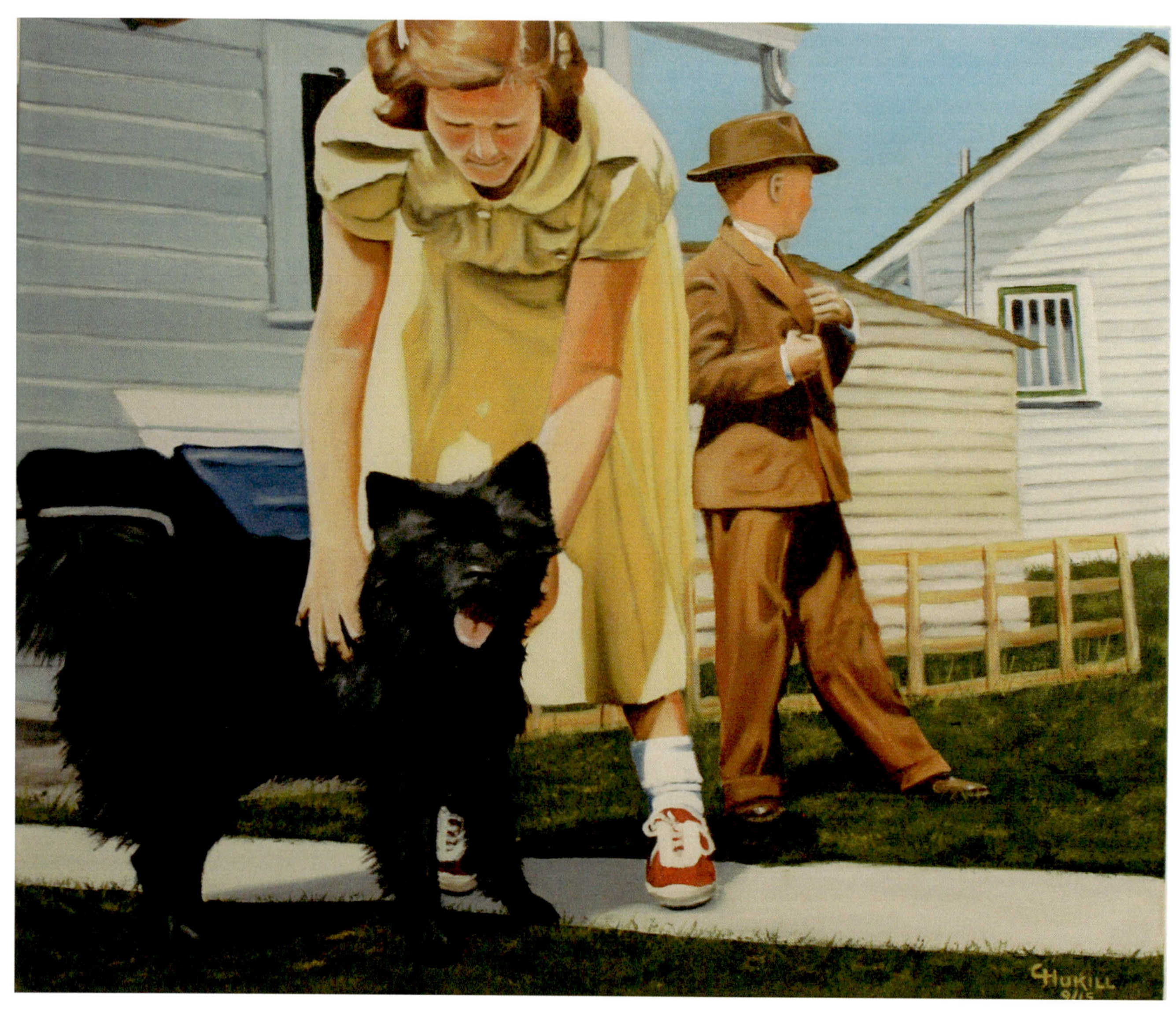

SMILE, 20X24

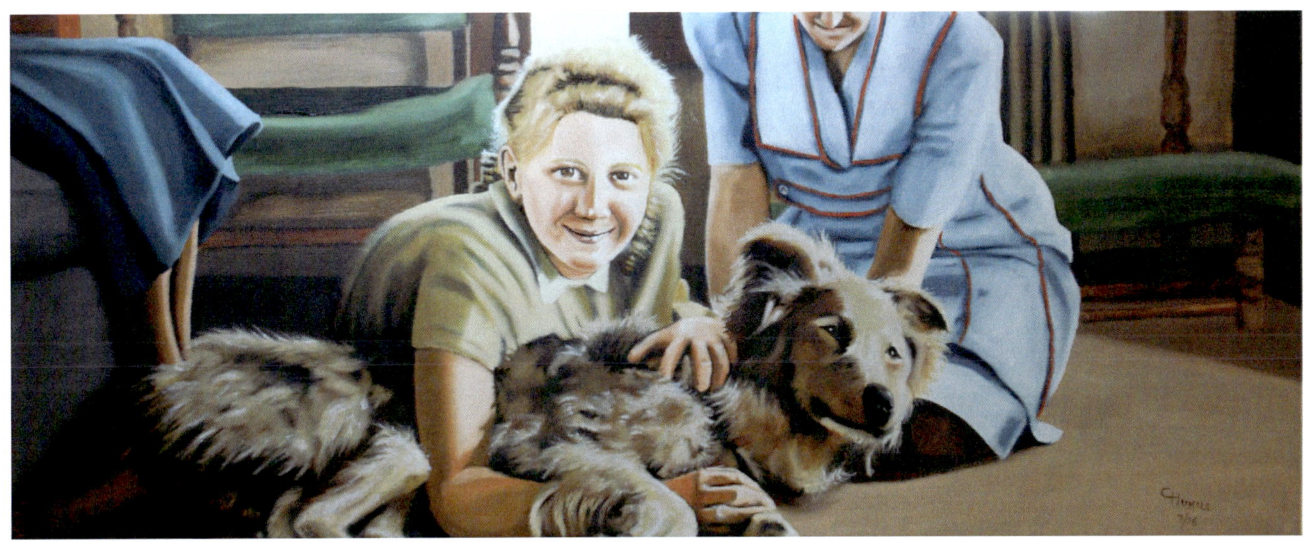

SHEER BLISS, 16X40*

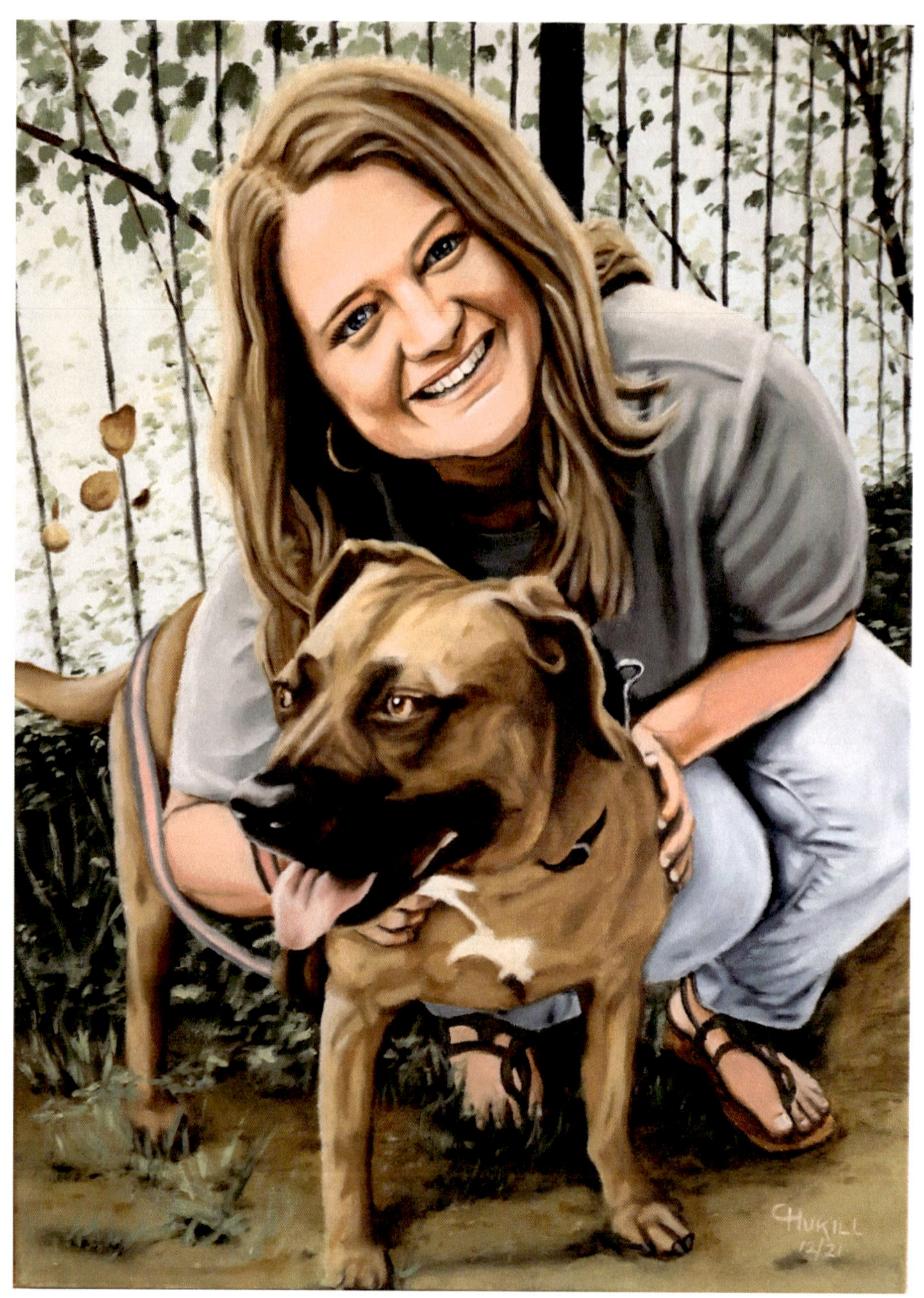

BEST BUDS, 18X24*

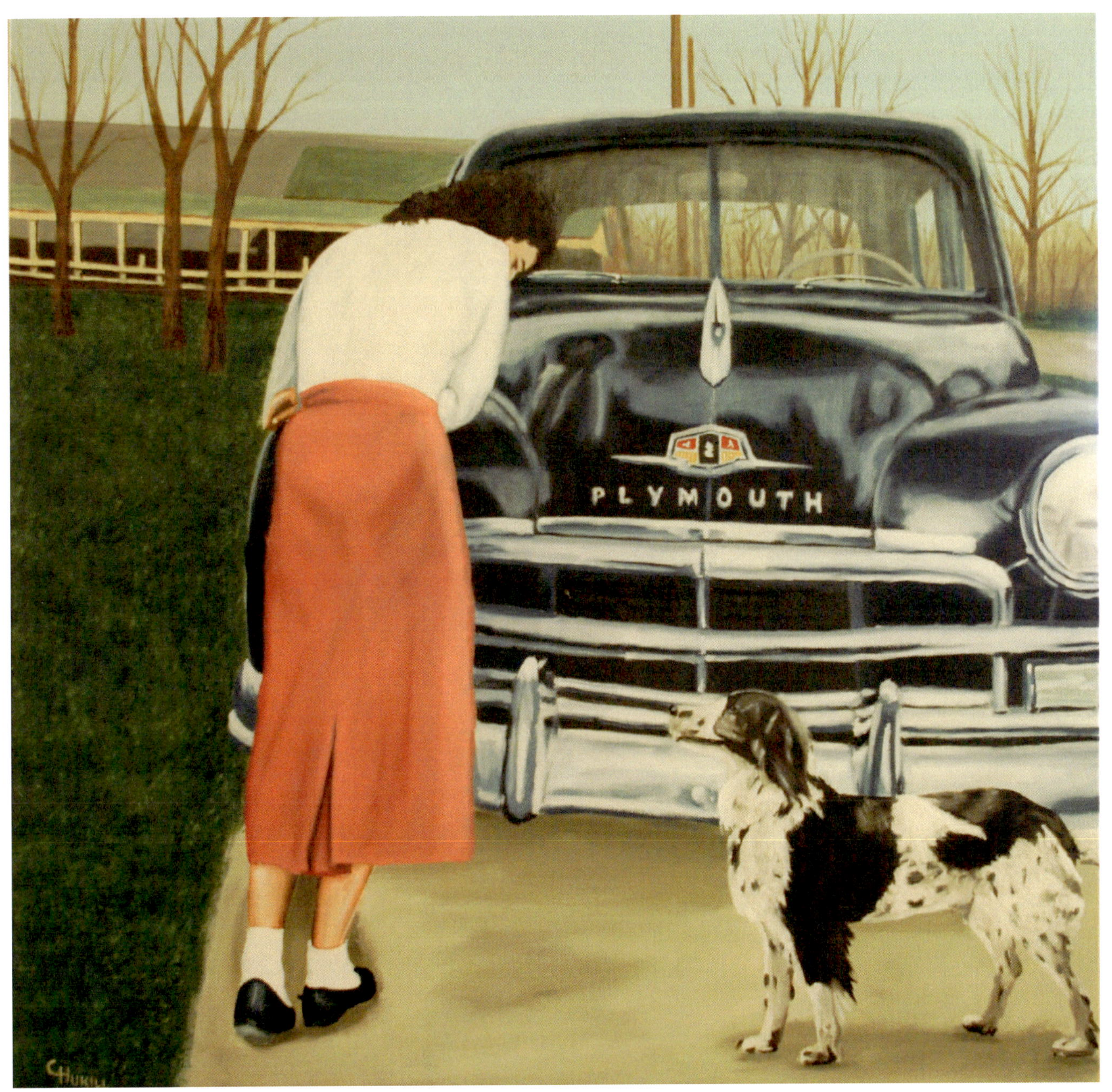

"WHAT?", 24X24*

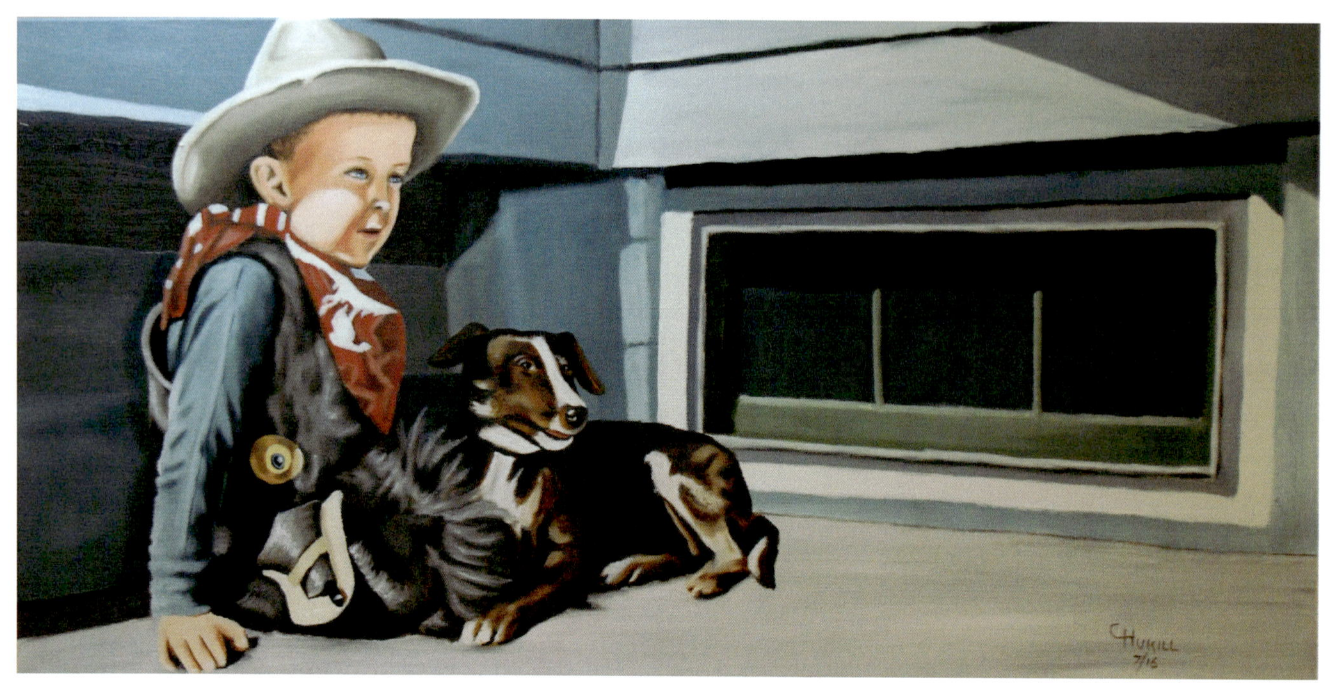

**TEX AND COWBOY, 15X30**

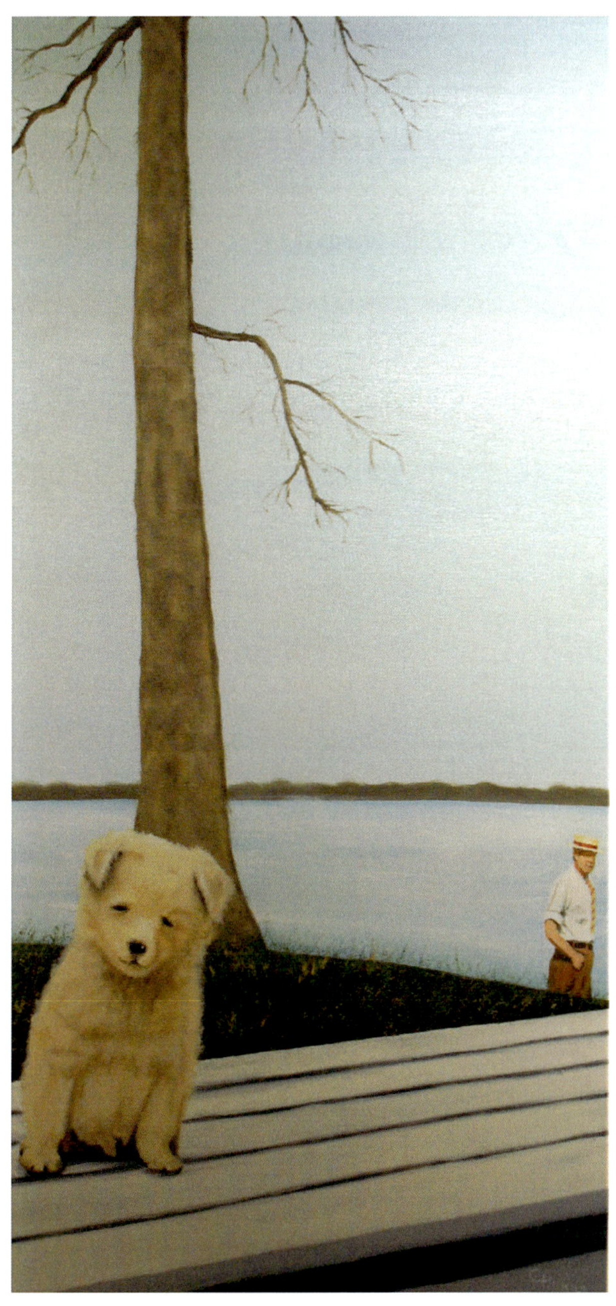

**HONEY BEAR, 15X30**

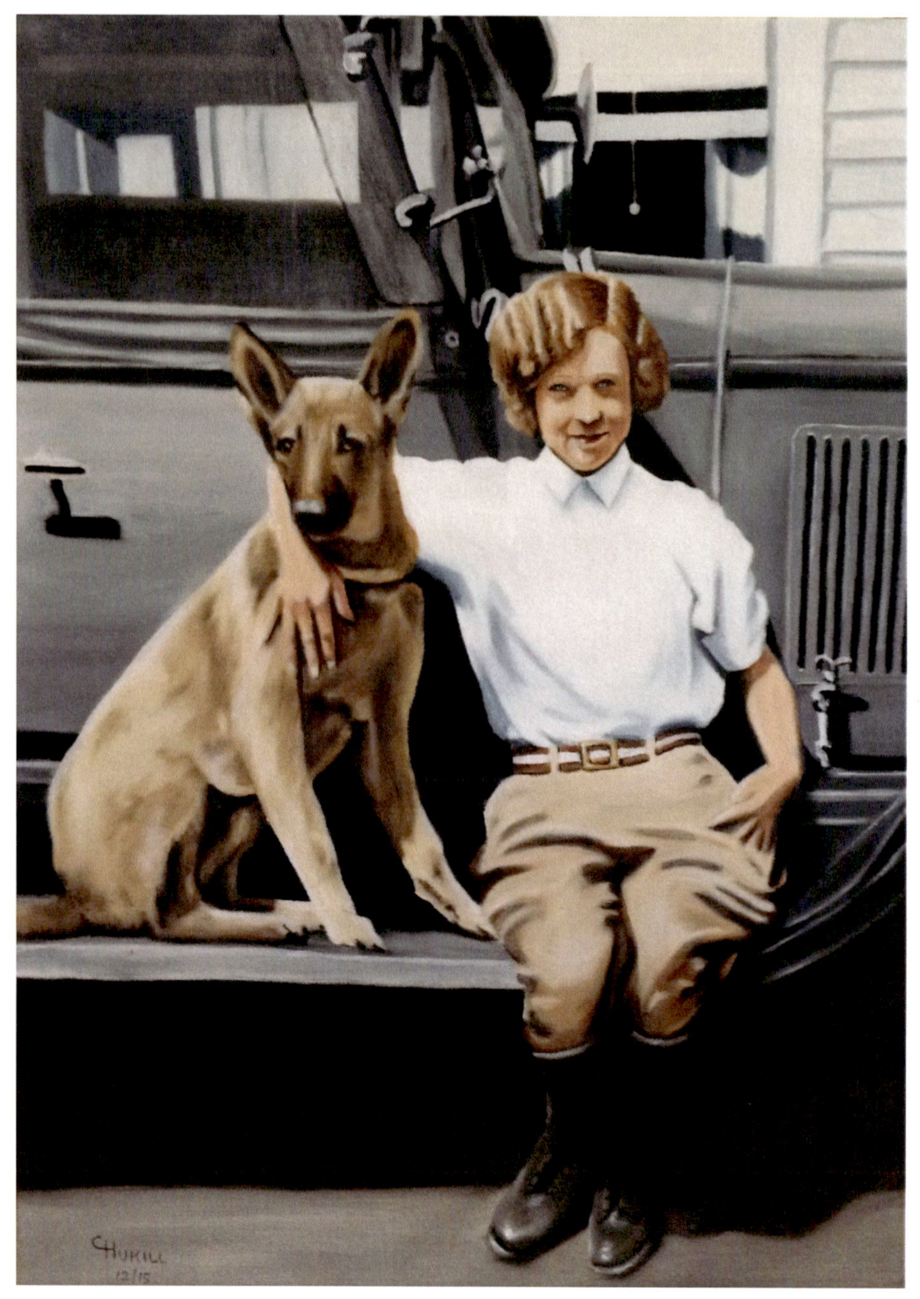

RUNNING BOARD BUDDIES, 18X24

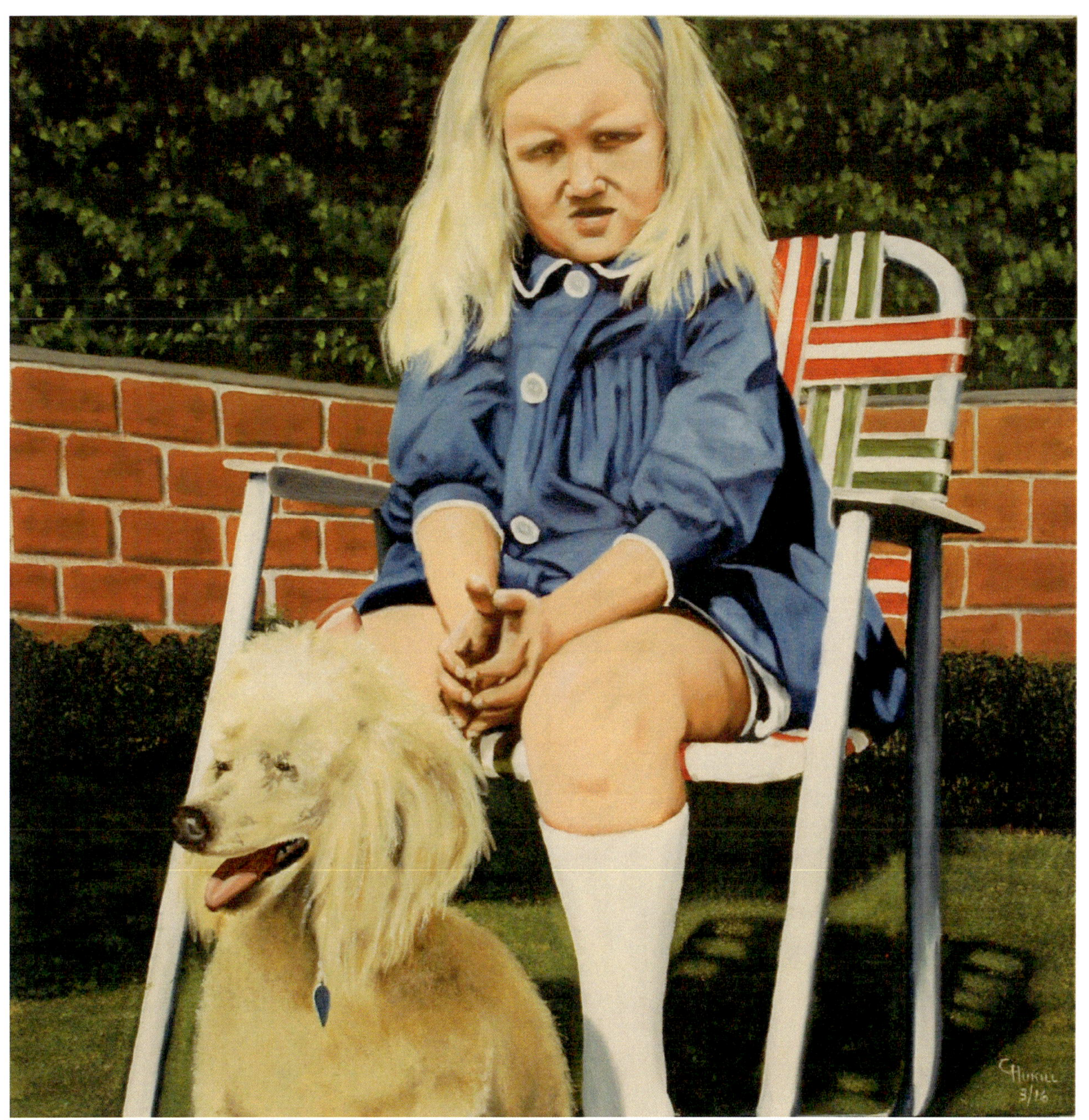

POODLE CUT, 24X24

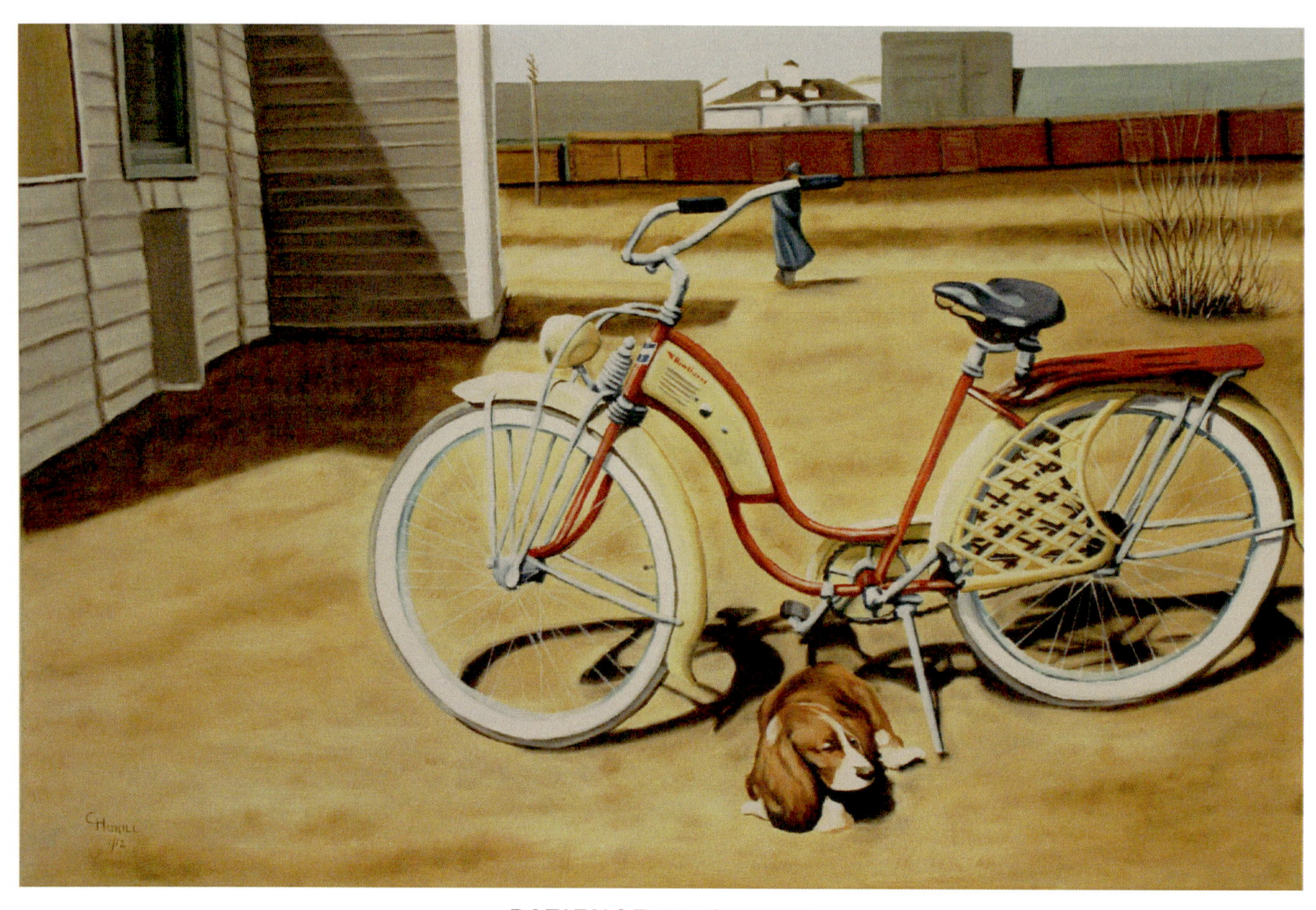

**PATIENCE #1, 24X36***

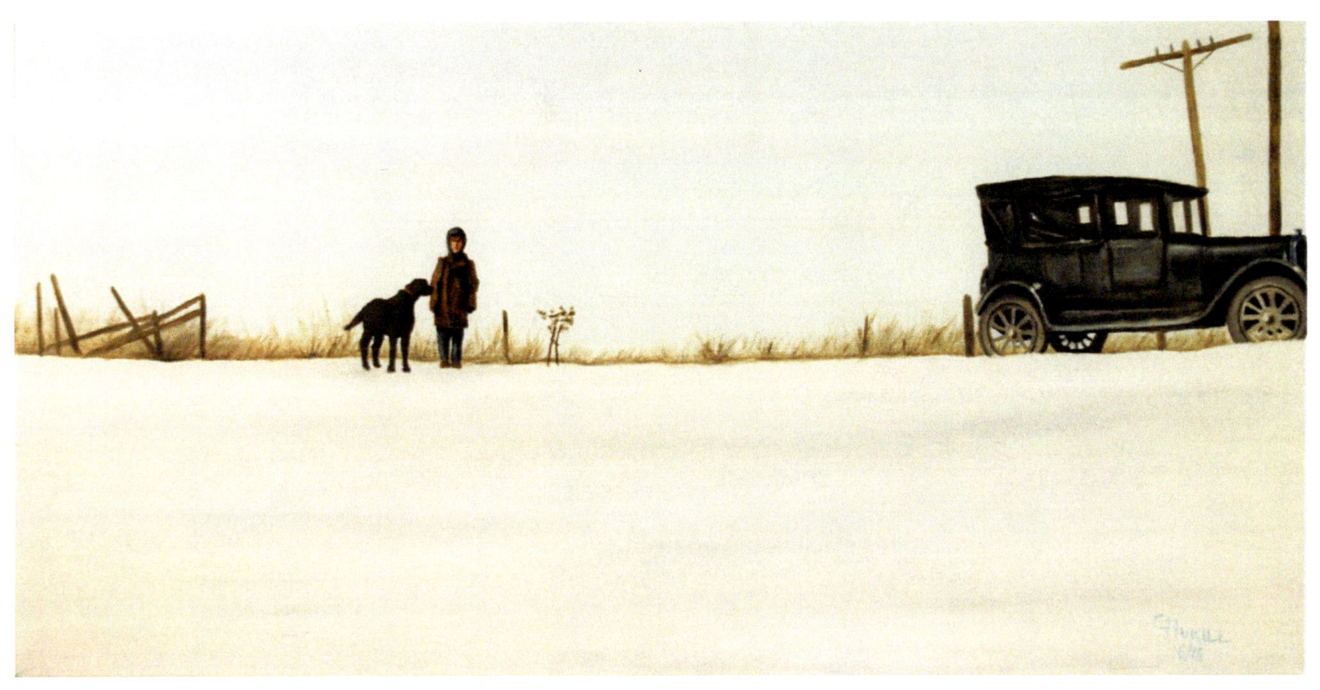

LOYALTY, 15X30*

# A Family of Friends

Many of the paintings in this section were commissioned by close friends, and the rest were done as gifts. I considered my friends to be extended Nuclear Family members.

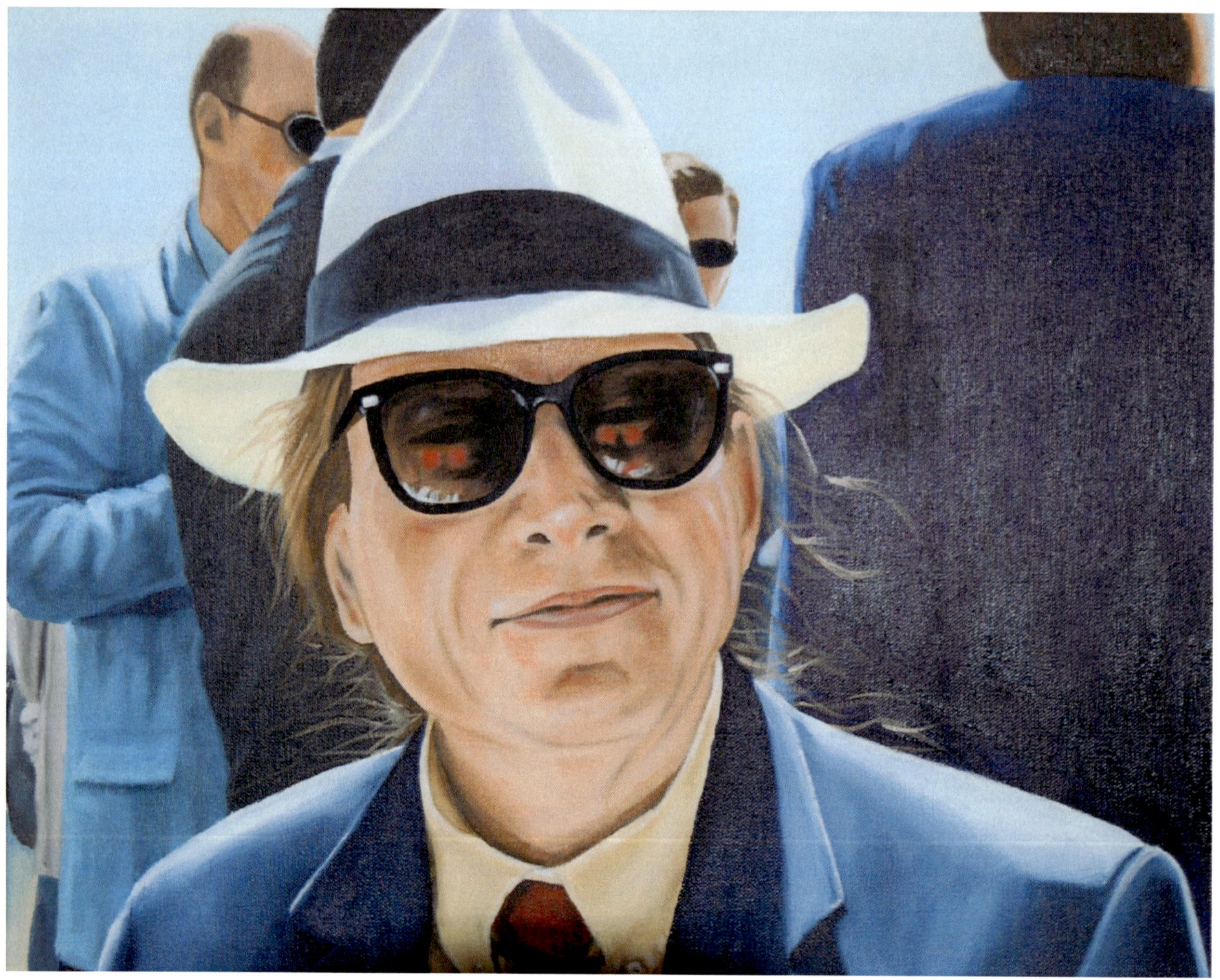

**JOHN: AT THE DERBY, 16X20***

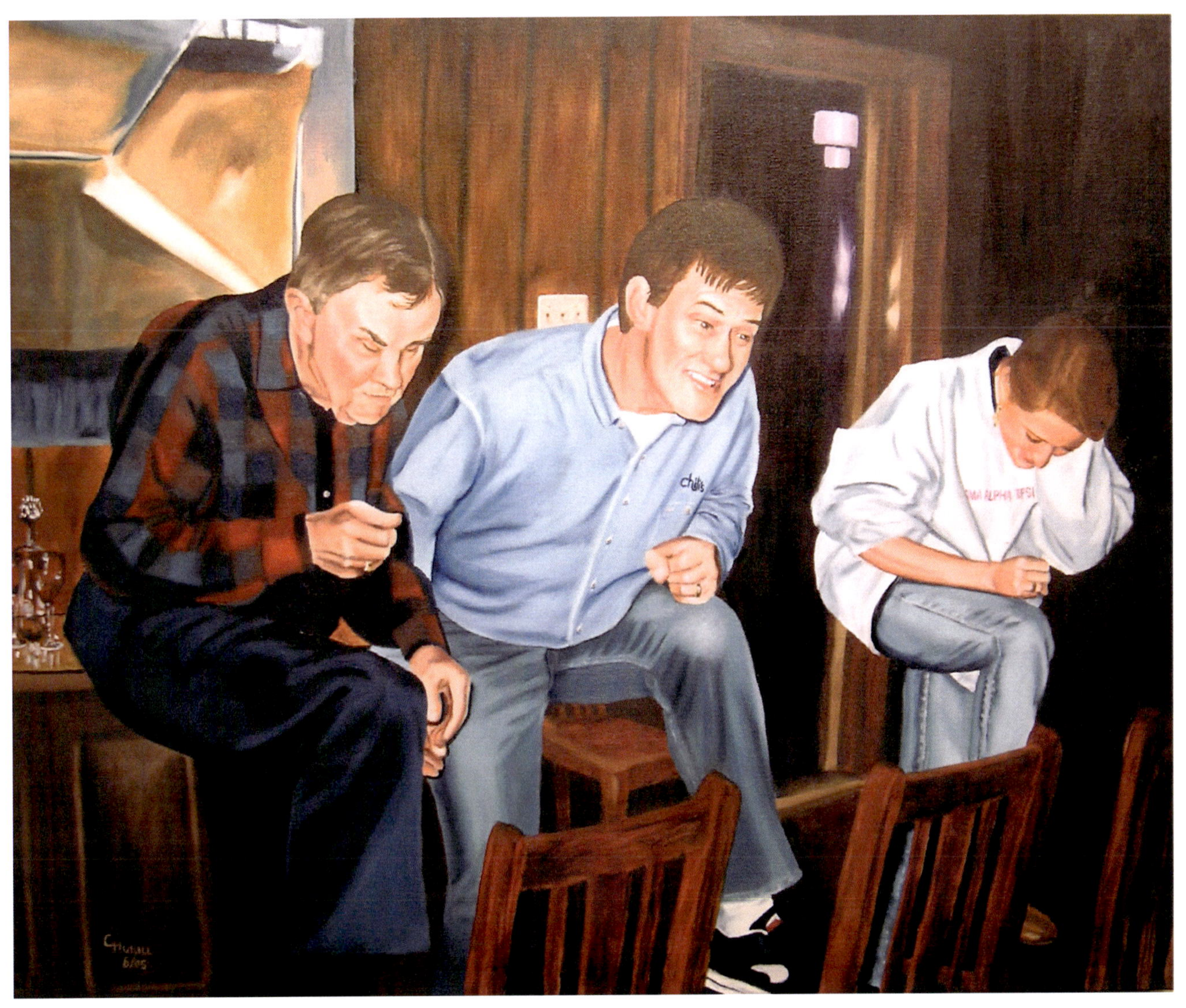

STUPID HUMAN TRICKS, 24X30*

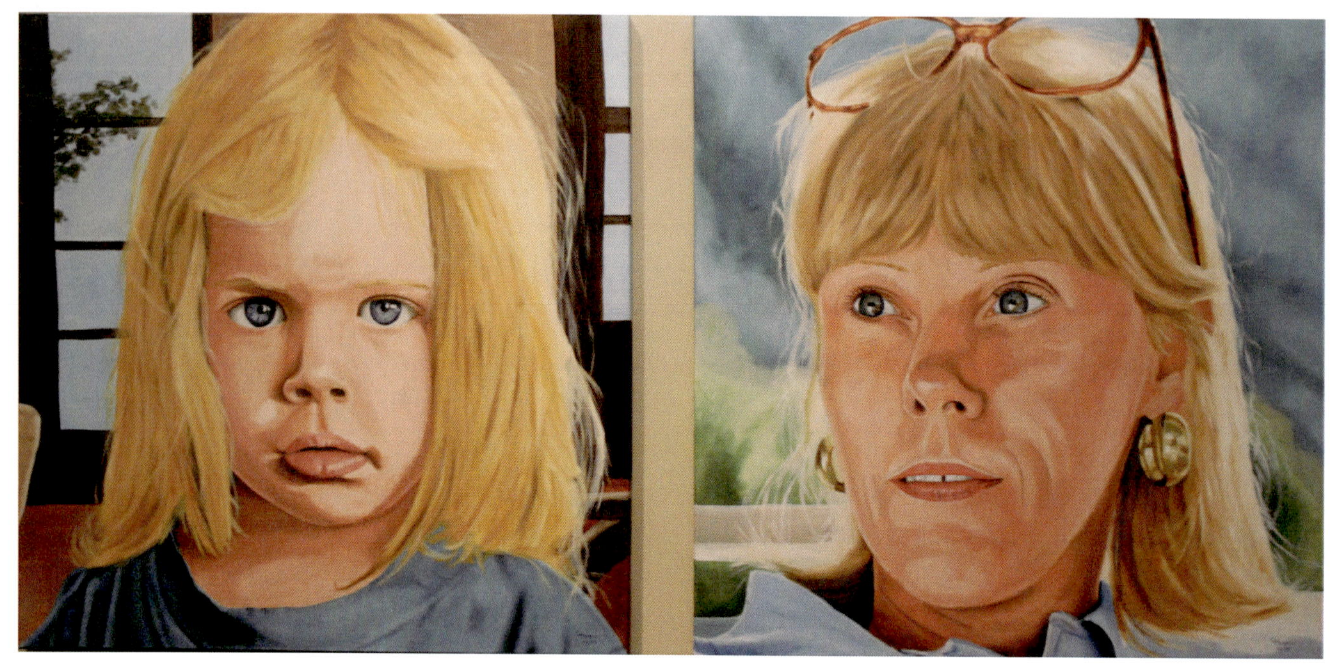

DIPTYCH: MAGGIE AND LAURIE, 30X30 EACH*

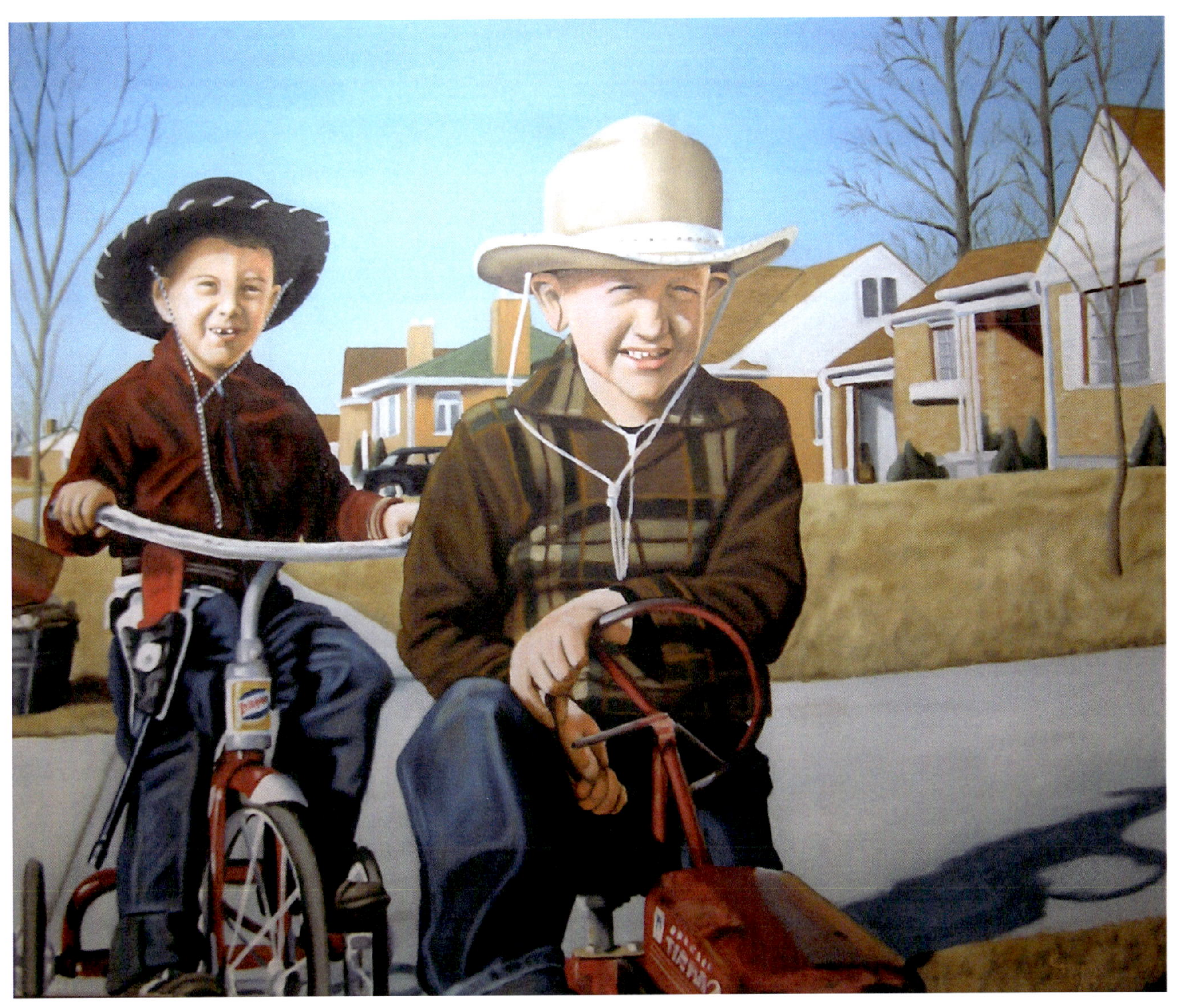

TRACTORS AND TRIKES, 18X24*

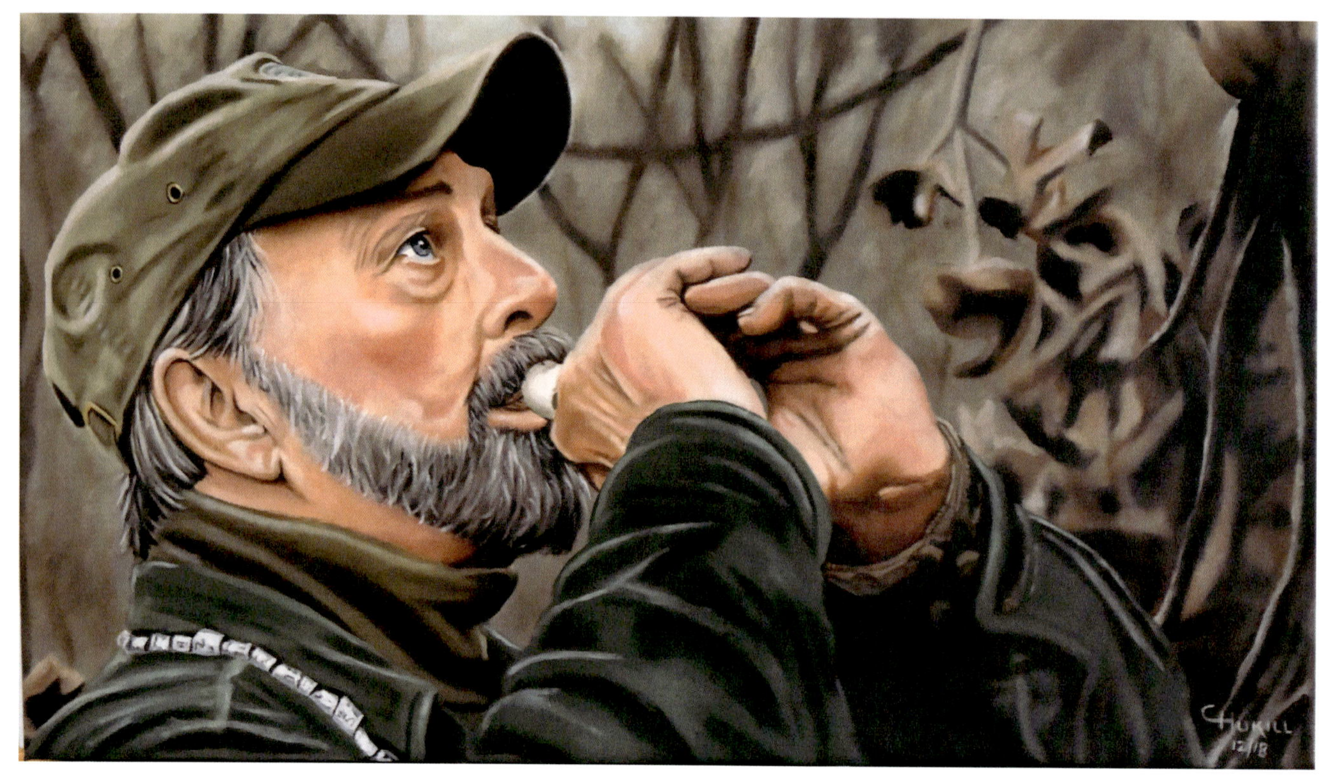

CALLING ALL DUCKS, 16X24*

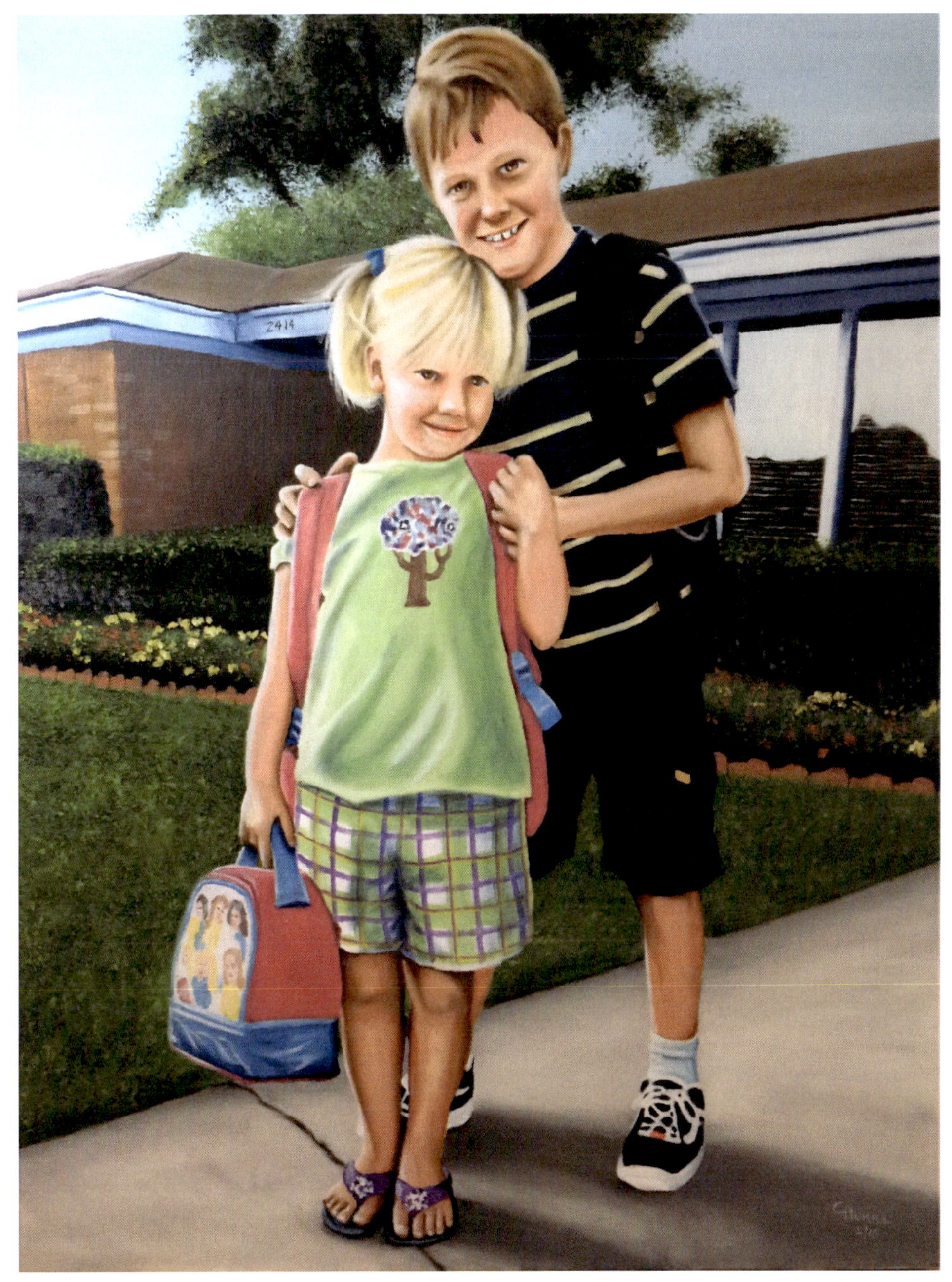

OFF TO SCHOOL, 18X24*

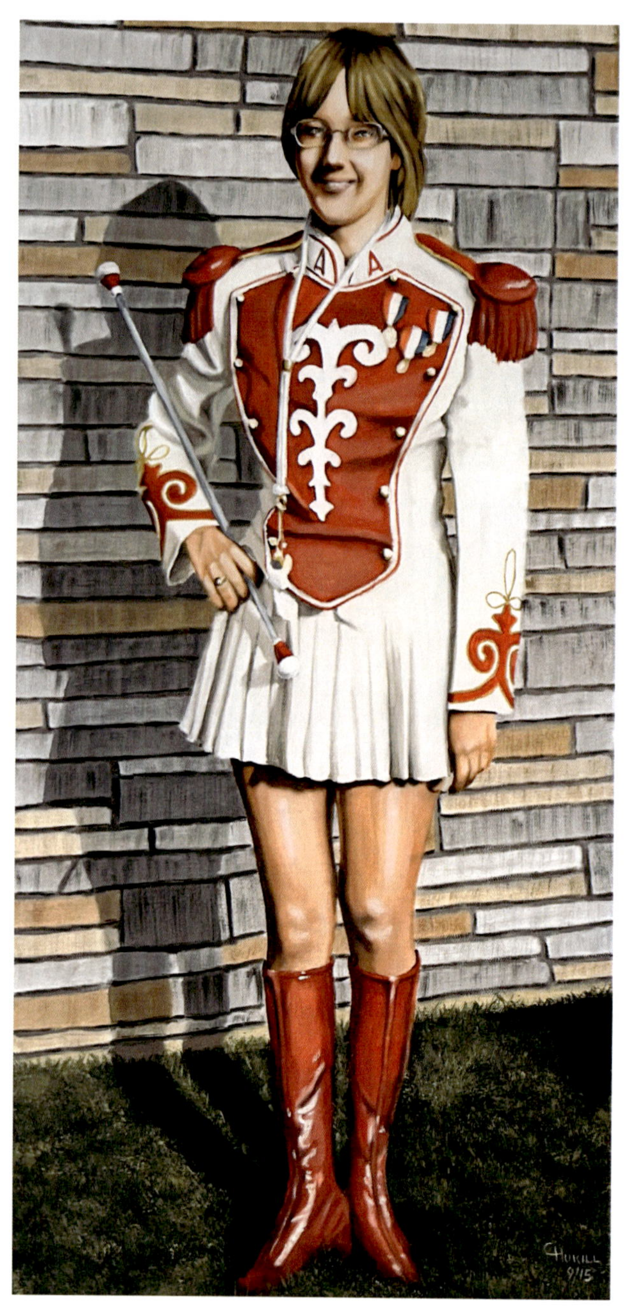

**CAROL MAY, 15X30***

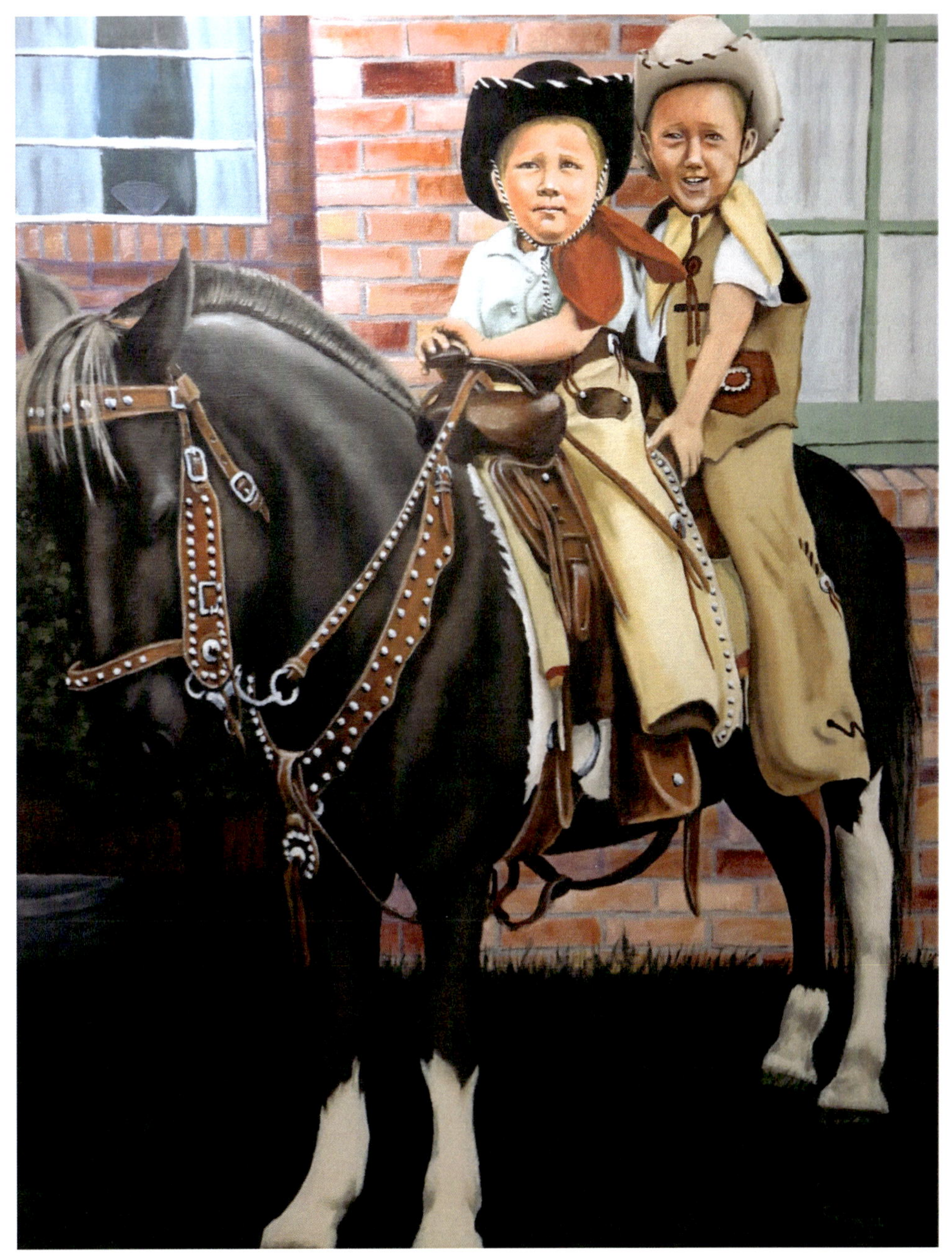

**MELODY AND DALE, 24X30***

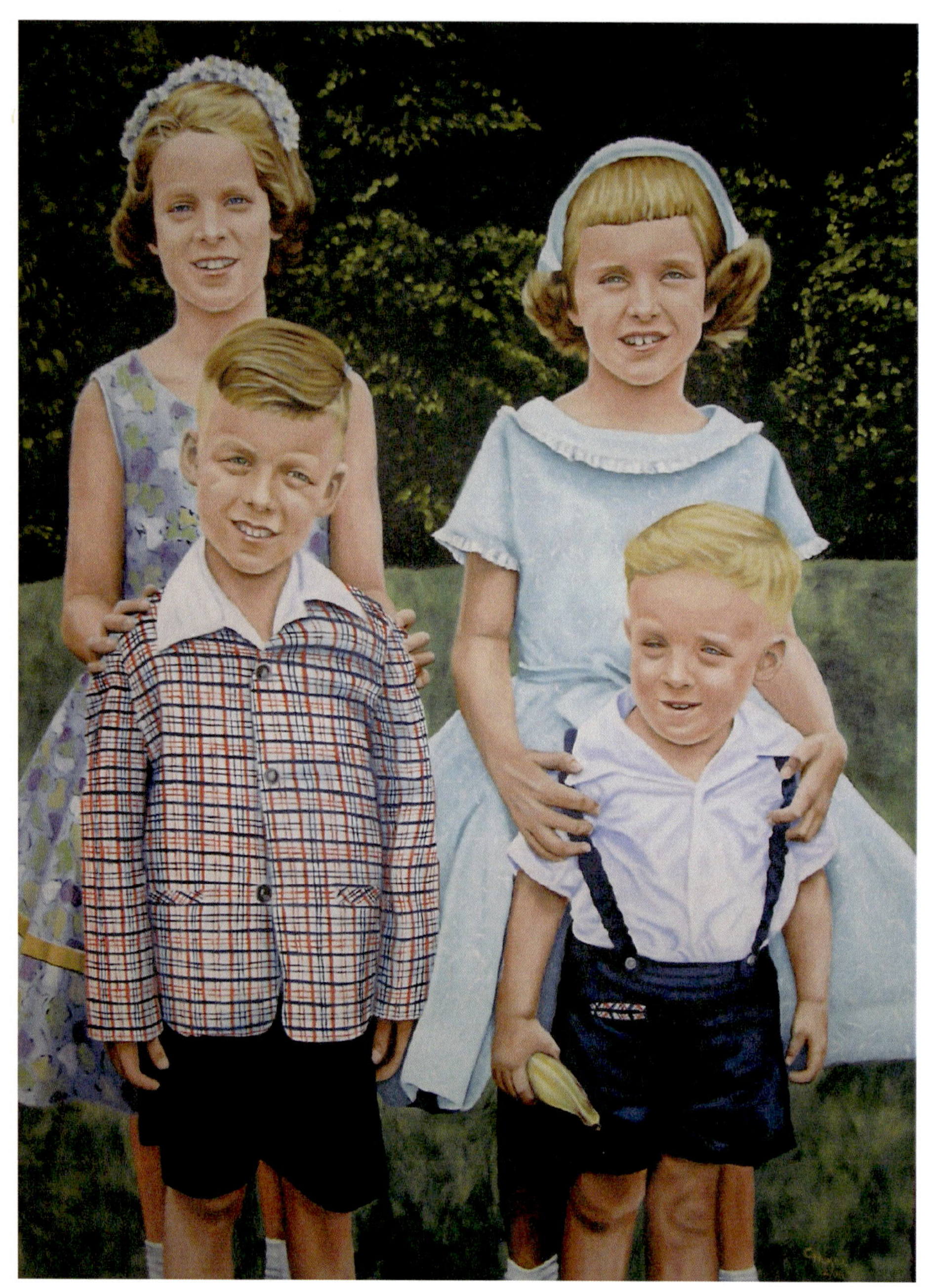

YES, WE HAVE A BANANA, 24X36*

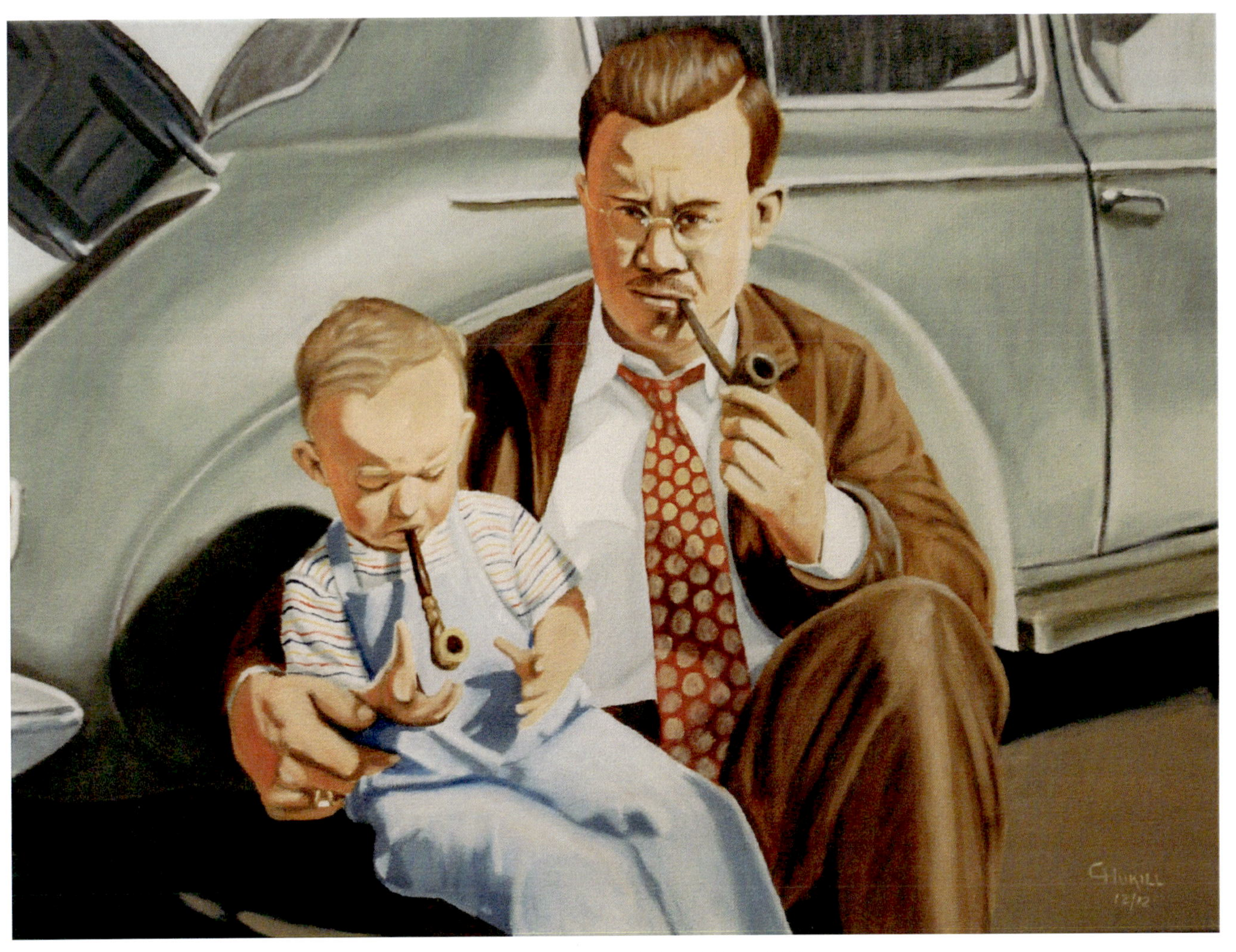

TRYING TO BE LIKE DAD, 18X24*

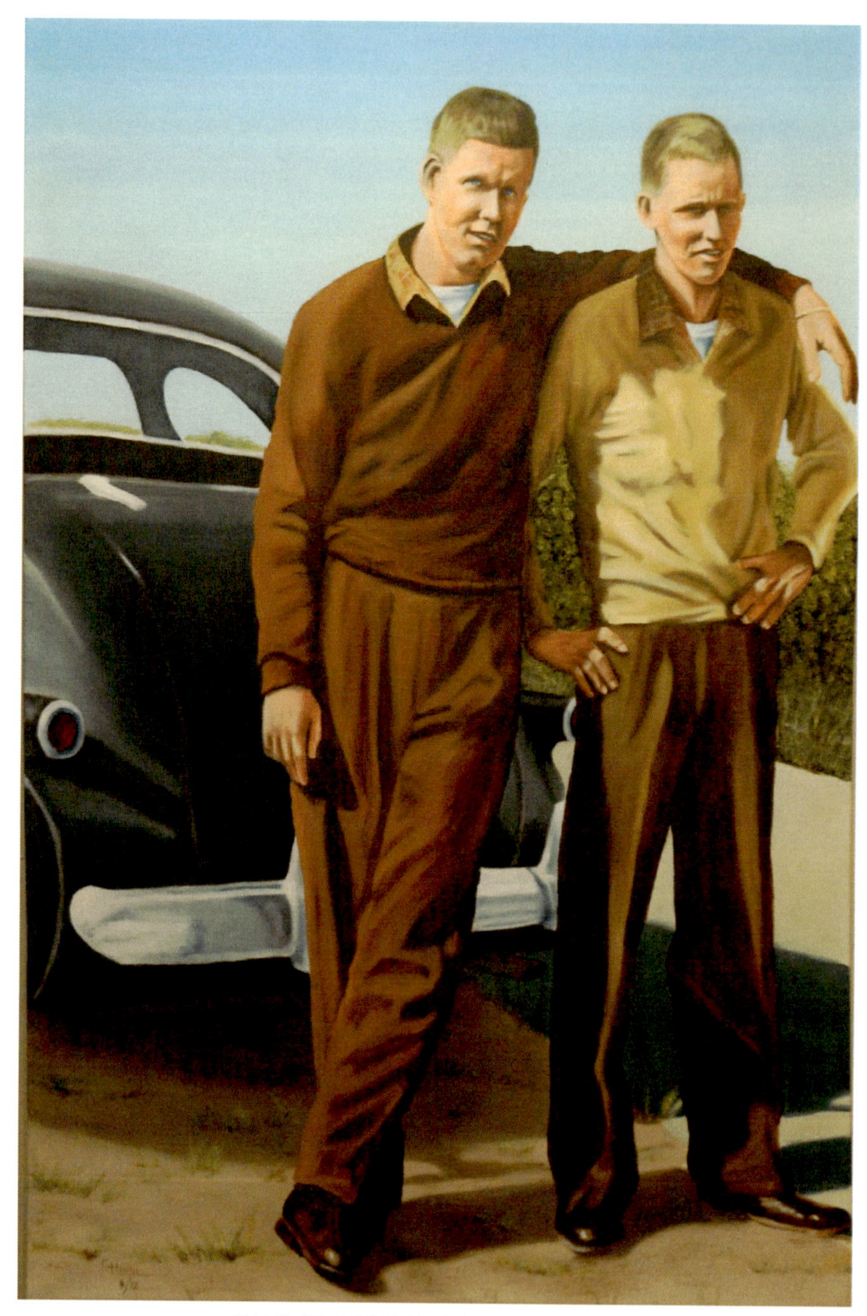

**THE ELLISON BOYS, 24X36***

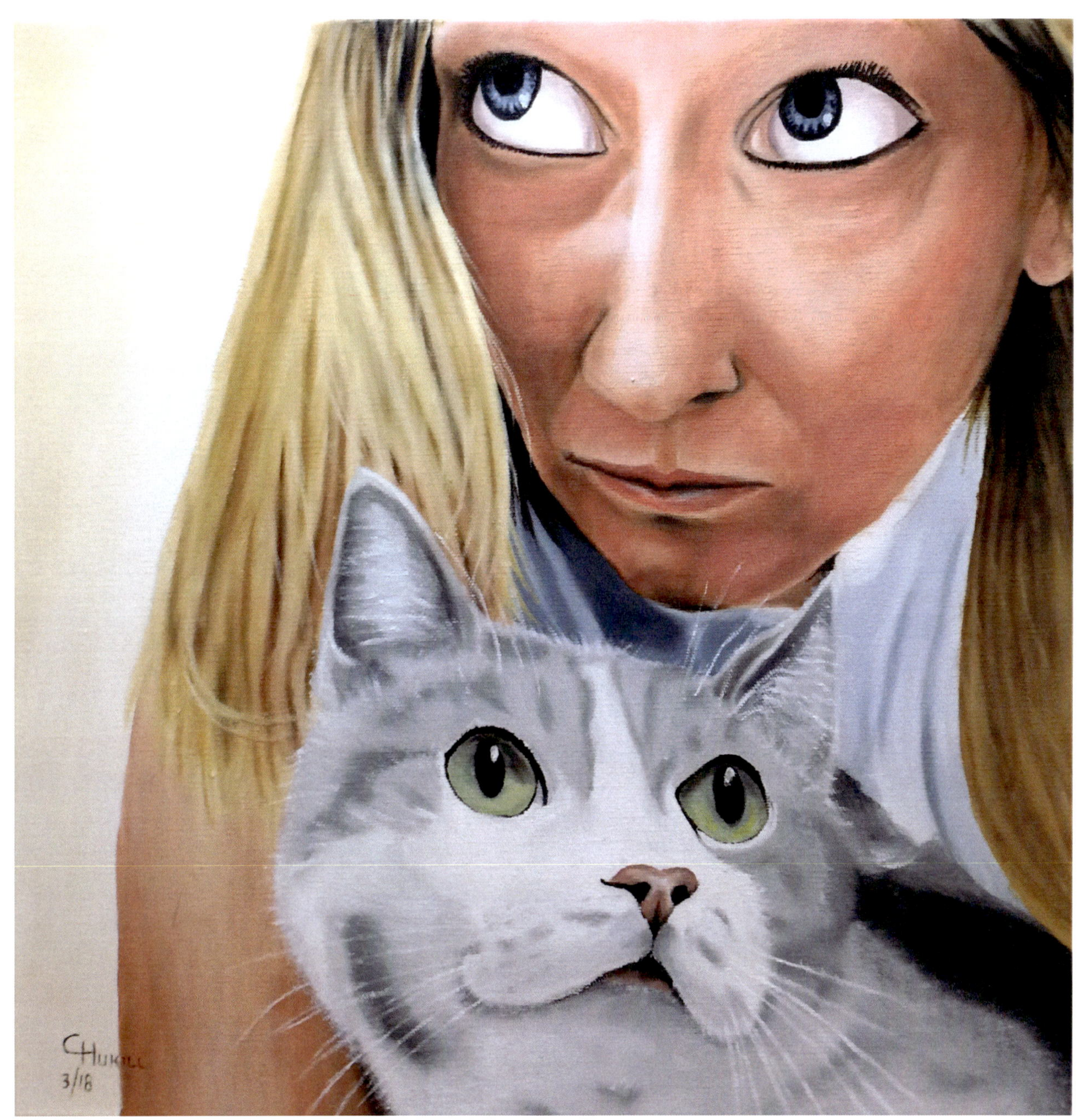

THE EYES HAVE IT, 20X20*

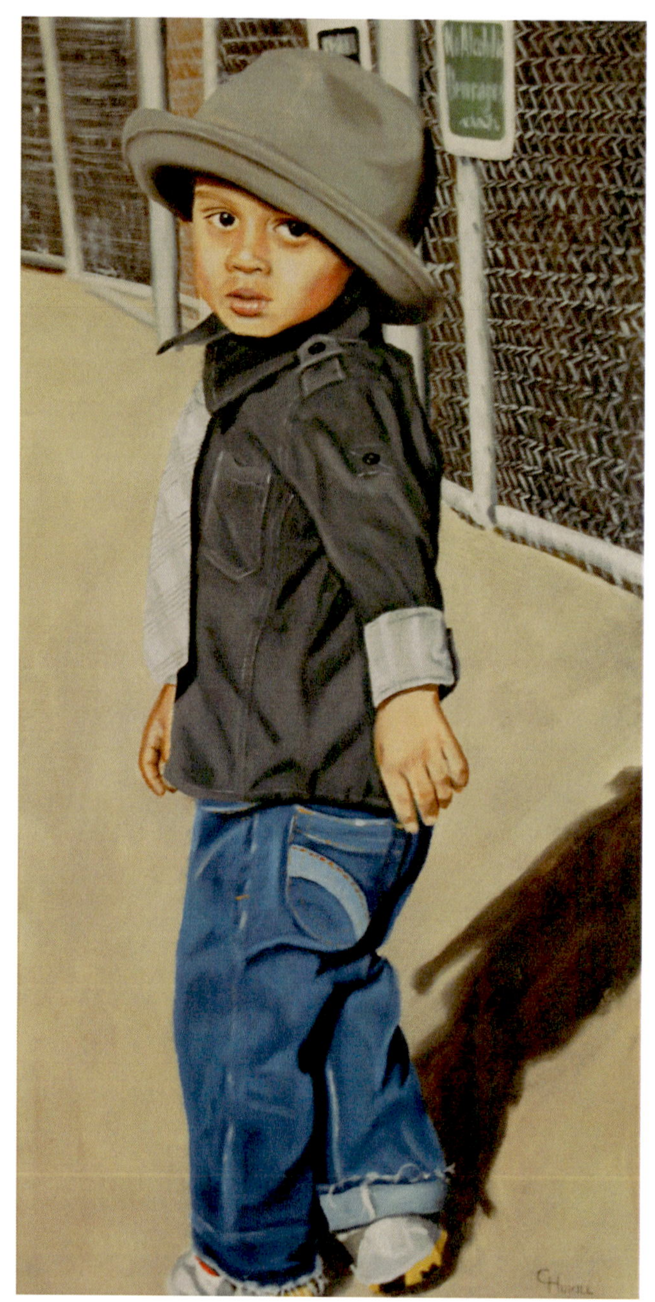

XAVI, 15X30*

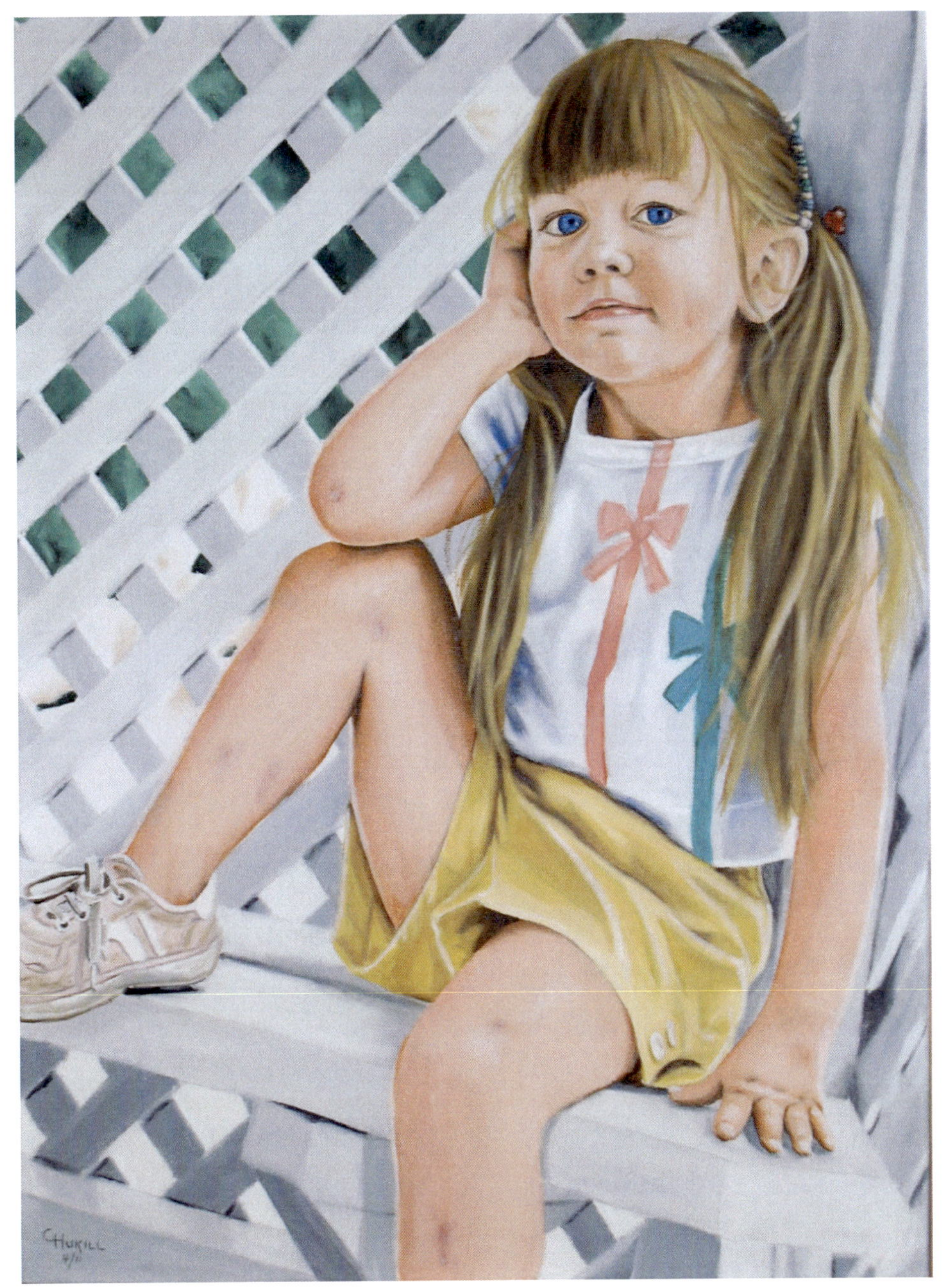

**BRUISES AND ALL, 18X24***

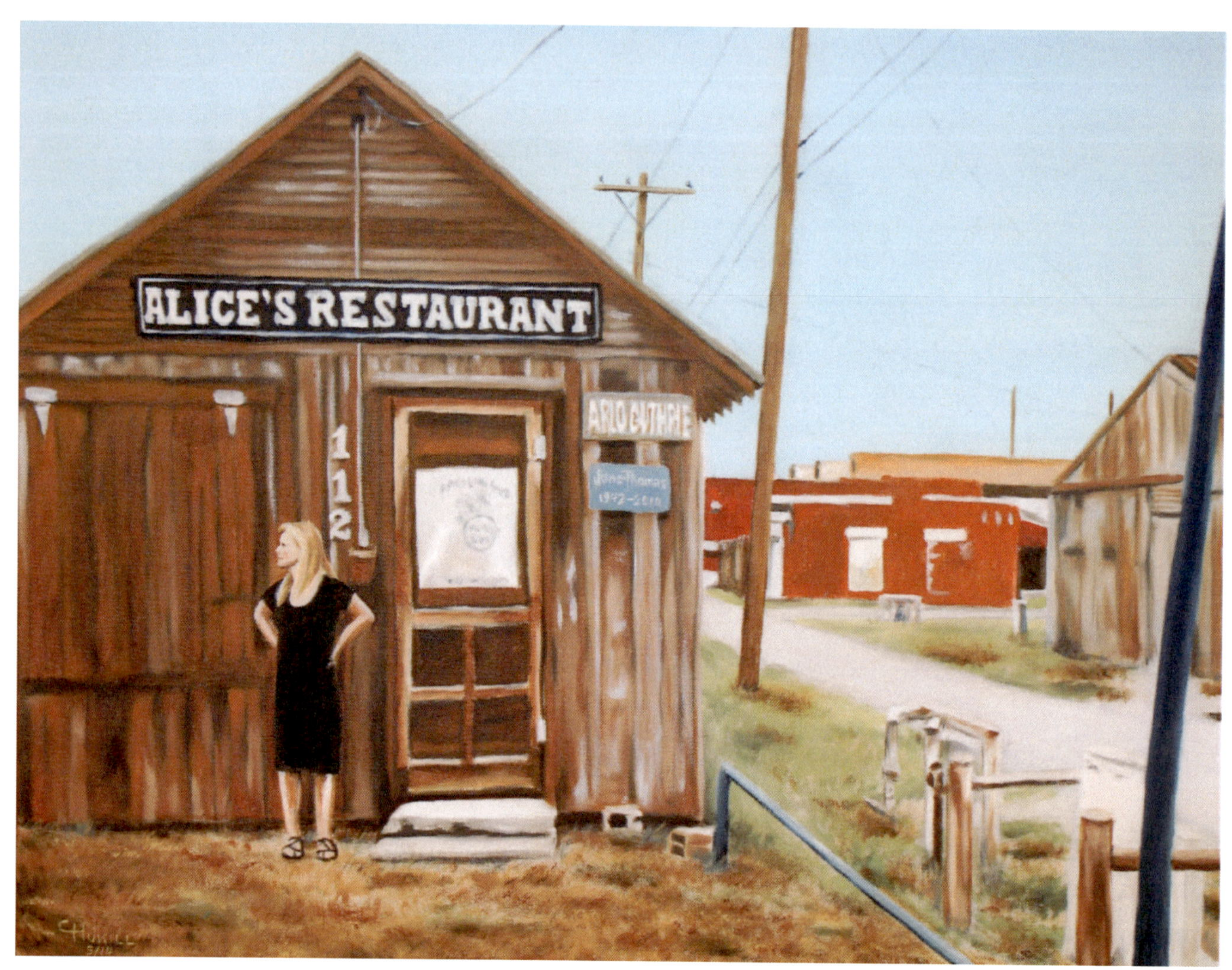


GUTHRIE, 16X20*

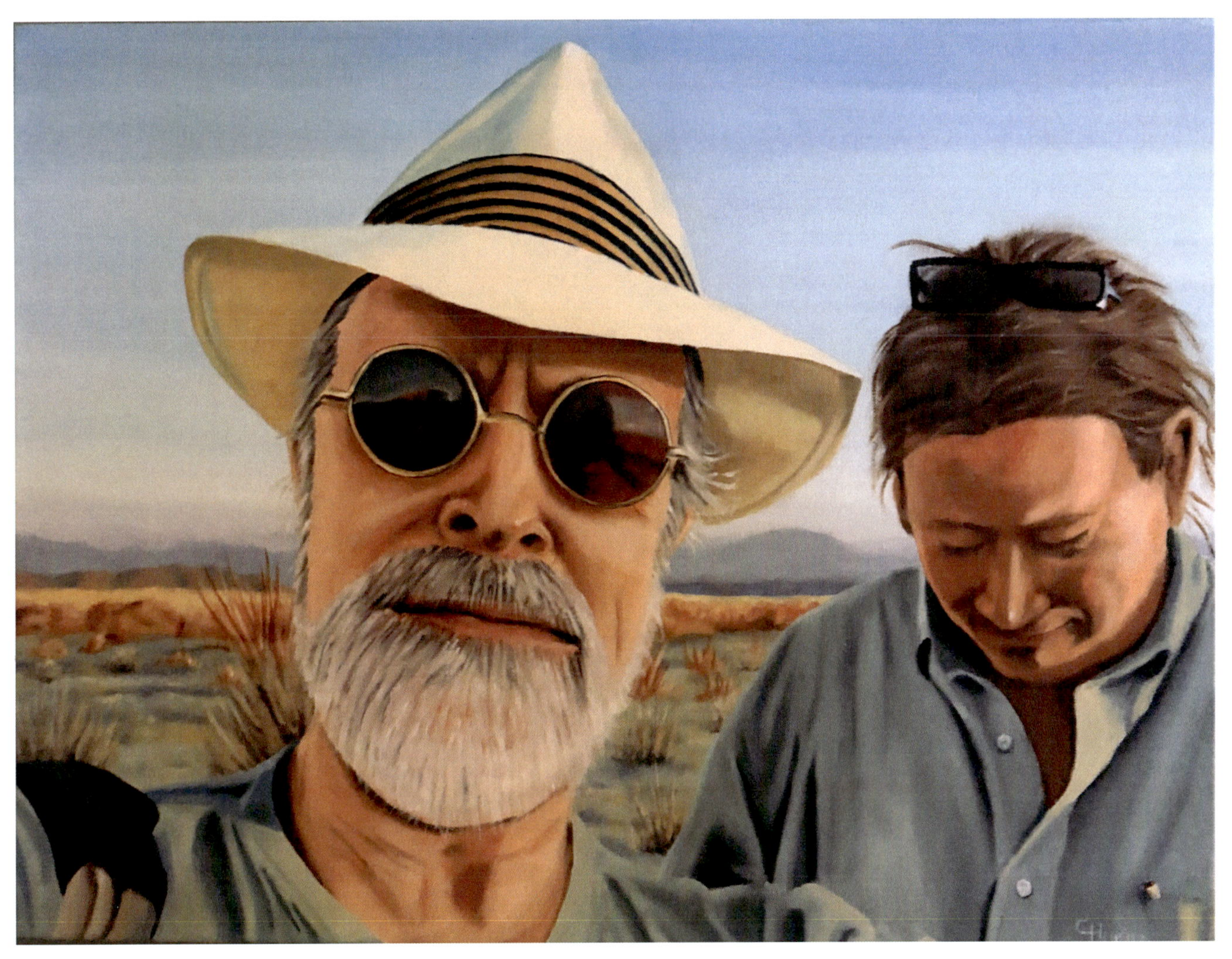

SELF-PORTRAIT WITH JOHN: WAITING ON THE MARFA LIGHTS, 18X24*

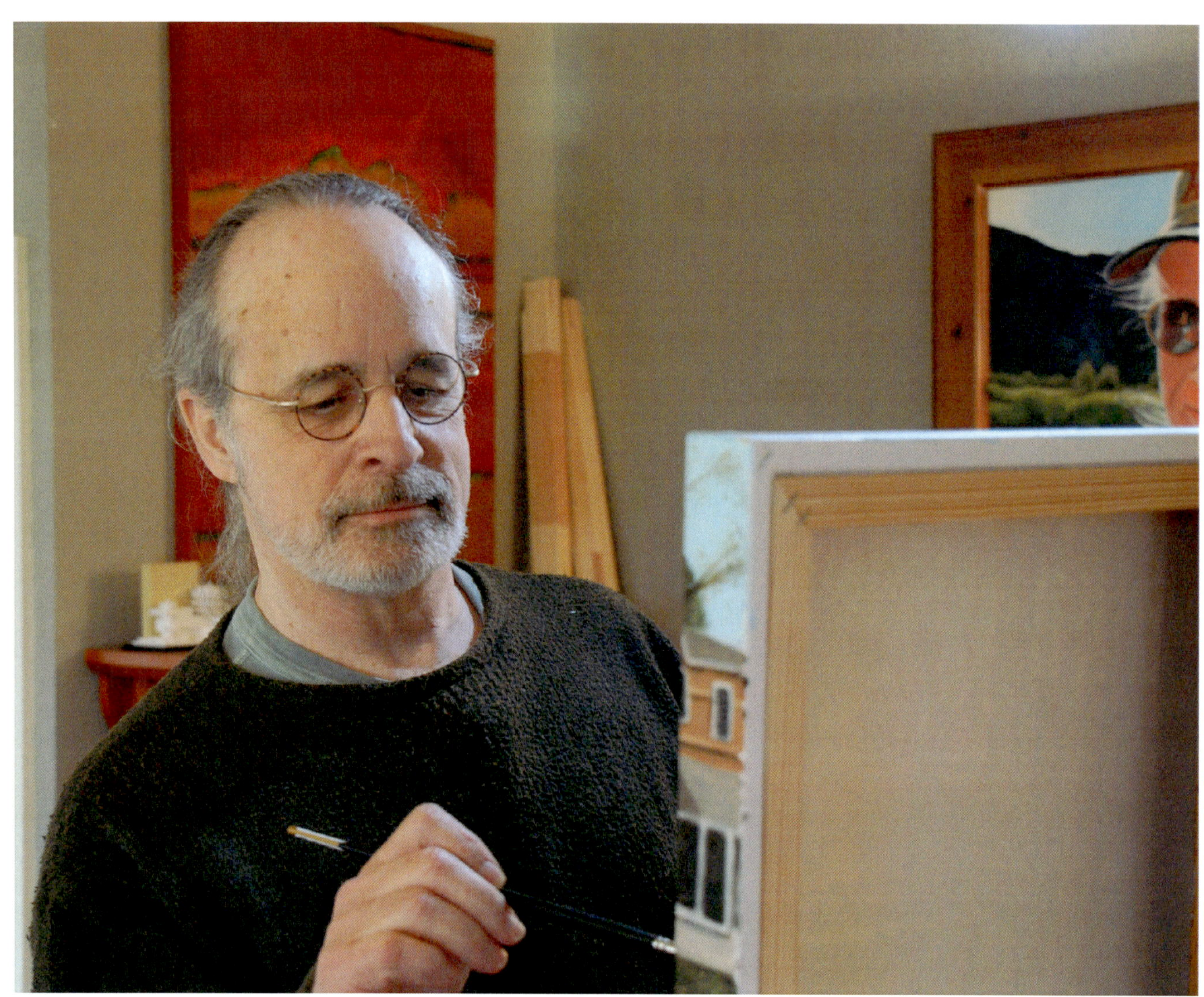

# About the Artist

Charlie Hukill is Professor Emeritus of Theatre at McMurry University where he designed and built scenery and designed and executed lighting for stage productions. He holds a BFA in Theatre from Stephen F. Austin State University, an MFA in Design and Playwriting from Trinity University, with an additional sixty hours of post-graduate study in Fine Arts from Texas Tech University.

Charlie has been pursuing artistic endeavors as long as he can remember and began painting in oils while a student in junior high in 1966. He studied oil painting for three years at the Fort Worth Museum of Modern Art under W.C. Austin and would rather paint than just about anything else. He has been a Signature Artist Member of the Center for Contemporary Arts since the Artist League of Texas days. Charlie has had six exhibits in the Jane Breed Gallery of the CCA -- four were solo and two were with friends. He has also had one exhibition in the Upstairs Gallery at the CCA, two exhibitions at the River Oaks Gallery, and one at McMurry University.

Recognitions at McMurry include the Outstanding Faculty of the Year (2000), the Graduates' Faculty Award (2001), the Gordon R. and Lola J. Bennett Award (2002), and the E.E. Hall Memorial Scholarship Award (2005). Most recently both he and Betty were awarded Honorary Doctor of Arts Degrees. In addition, he was recognized as the 2017 Stephen F. Austin Distinguished Theatre Alumnus. In 2023, he was included as one of the McMurry 100.

He is married to the lovely and talented Betty Hukill and they have immersed themselves wholeheartedly into retirement.

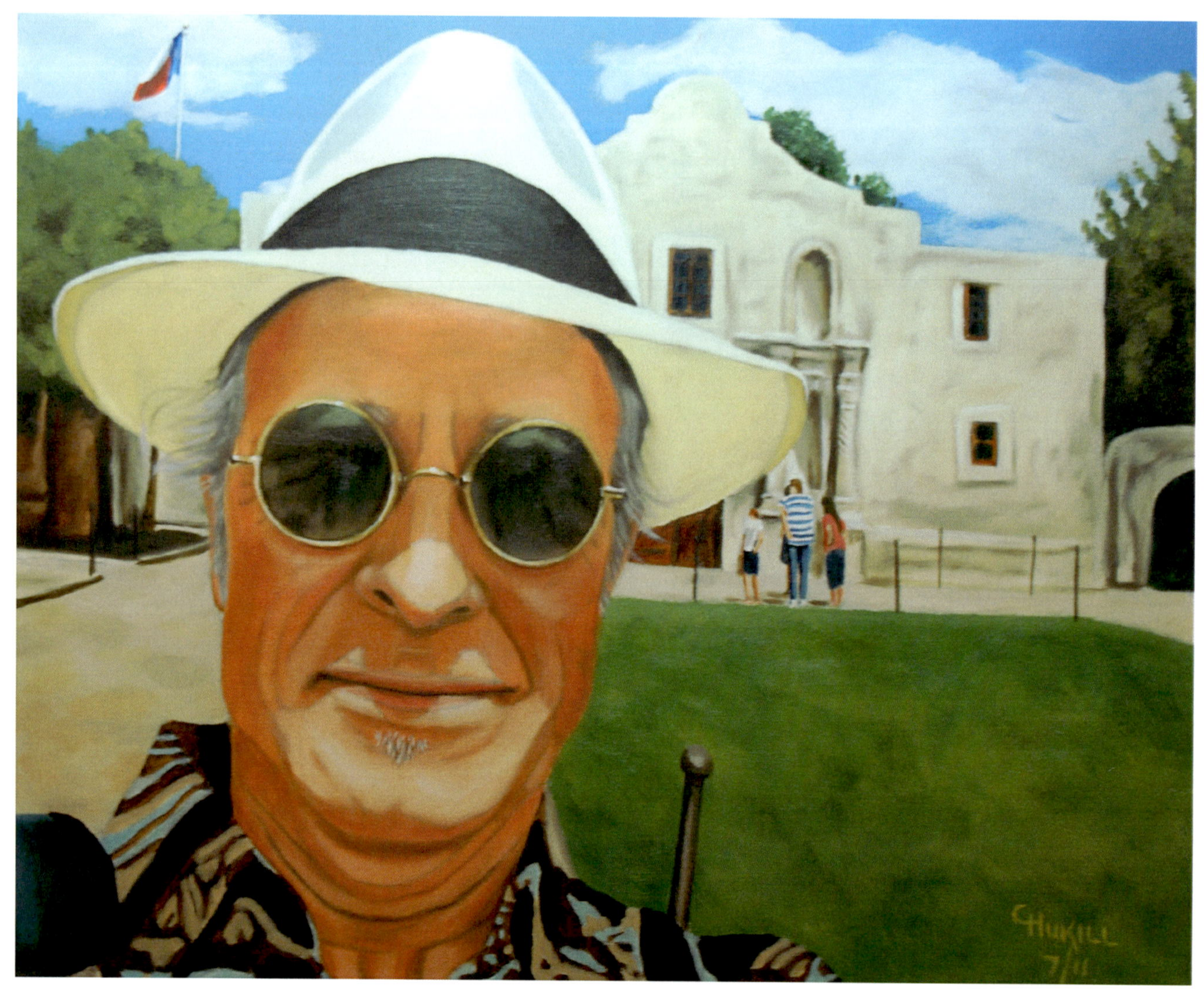

**SELF-PORTRAIT AT THE ALAMO, 16X20***

For more paintings by Charlie Hukill, see his web site: charliehukill.com

www.ingramcontent.com/pod-product-compliance
Lightning Source LLC
Chambersburg PA
CBRC090746110726
48005CB00008B/977